Søren Kierkegaard: The Mystique Of Prayer And Pray-er

Translated and Published by
Special Permission of

Det kongelige Bibliotek
Copenhagen, Denmark

Translated by Lois S. Bowers
Edited by George K. Bowers

CSS Publishing Company, Inc.
Lima, Ohio

Copyright © 1994 by
CSS Publishing Company, Inc.
Lima, Ohio

Scripture quotations are from the *Revised Standard Version of the Bible,* copyrighted 1946, 1952 (c), 1973, by the Division of Christian Education of the National Council of the Churches of Christ in the USA. Used by permission.

Library of Congress Cataloging-in-Publication Data

Kierkegaard, Soren, 1813-1855.
    The mystique of prayer and pray-er / Soren Kierkegaard; translated by Lois S. Bowers; edited by George K. Bowers.
        p.   cm.
    "By special permission of Det kongelige Bibliotek ... Copenhagen."
    Includes bibliographical references.
    ISBN 0-7880-0301-1
    1. Prayers. 2. Prayer—Christianity. I. Bowers, George K., 1915-   . II. Title.
BV245.K54   1994
242'.8—dc20
                                                                94-29859
                                                                CIP

This book is available in the following formats, listed by ISBN:
0-7880-0301-1 Book
0-7880-0302-X IBM 3 1/2 computer disk
0-7880-0303-8 IBM 3 1/2 book and disk package
0-7880-0304-6 Macintosh computer disk
0-7880-0305-4 Macintosh book and disk package
0-7880-0306-2 IBM 5 1/4 computer disk
0-7880-0307-0 IBM 5 1/4 book and disk package

PRINTED IN U.S.A.

DEDICATED to the faculty and administration (past and present) of Gettysburg College for the cultural and intellectual treasures that they have bequeathed to us and to countless others through the years!

Table Of Contents

Foreword

Since the days as a graduate student in theology when Kierkegaard's writings first appeared in English translation, no one modern theologian has occupied more of my attention and delight. No one theologian — except perhaps Augustine or Luther — has more influenced the direction of my own theological thought as well as the theological works of those who have been my principal mentors. Kierkegaard's influence, so diversified, profound and controversial, has impacted philosophy, literature, psychology, the arts and, of course, theology. It is always a joy, therefore, to review a new and fresh work by and concerning the Danish thinker.

This little work by Lois and George Bowers is a timely and welcome addition to the already extensive Kierkegaardian library. It is one of the few, if any, offerings within the last forty years to deal with Kierkegaard's prayer and piety. Moreover, it is a spiritually penetrative book. It not only handles in translation selected prayers of Kierkegaard with adeptness and in contemporary idiom, but it applies his reflections in personal meditations which would have warmed the heart of the Danish master of religious inwardness. For Kierkegaard would have liked nothing better than to see his writings move others to spiritual reflection.

The Bowers, for the most part, have eschewed preoccupation with Kierkegaard's elaborate pilgrimage through the aesthetic, ethical and religious stages on life's way in order to "will one thing" in their book, that is, to deal with the interior prayer life of this man of faith. Further, as Kierkegaard himself insisted on moving beyond the objective meaning of Christianity to the subjective appropriation of it, so the Bowers' manuscript moves from the translated prayers of S.K. to prayerful application and spiritual exercises. The book, therefore, has a dual purpose: to make available in contemporary English Kierkegaard's own penetrating prayers, and to provide for the reader a series of prayers fashioned in Kierkegaardian thought and mode.

There is a double delight one takes in this book: the unstilted beauty of the prayers themselves in translation, geared to the modern reader, and the sensitive understanding of those prayers incorporated into a series of meditations and prayers certain to uplift the reader.

Perhaps what pleased this reviewer most about this book was the way in which the authors caught up the salient elements in Kierkegaard's piety and practice of prayer. For example, the dialectical element, present in all of S.K.'s thought, is prominent as well in his understanding of prayer. The pray-er who is aware of his own sin and unworthiness feels the distance, the infinite distance, between himself and God, and yet sensing that distance knows, too, that God is infinitely near with His infinite love. So, as unacceptable as one is before God, one knows nonetheless God's acceptance of the sinner. For Paul Tillich, himself profoundly influenced by Kierkegaard's theology, salvation is man's acceptance of that divine acceptance.

Again, the authors of this book consider Kierkegaard's wrestling with the difficulty and struggle of prayer. For one who has not engaged in *true* prayer the struggle may not be evident. But for the pray-er who earnestly desires an intimate relationship with God (true prayer), prayer is an increasing struggle. Yet, in the struggle the pray-er conquers because God ultimately conquers in bringing the pray-er to what he was created to be.

The Bowers capture other elements in Kierkegaard's life in and reflection on prayer: the filial relationship of God and the one who prays; the unconditional self-surrender in prayer; prayer as "willing, one thing" namely, God's will; prayer as silent waiting before God; God's unchangeable love and faithfulness which inwardly transforms the one who prays; the correlation between public prayer and individual participation in it.

Though relatively brief, the Bowers' book is well-conceived and balanced; first, just enough of an introduction to provide a helpful setting for an entrance into Kierkegaard's prayers and fragments of his theological reflection on prayer; then a series of commentaries on Kierkegaard's prayer reflections followed by a selection of contemporary and penetrating prayers in an existential mode which no doubt would have delighted immensely the Danish theologian.

We are grateful to the Bowers for this timely piece on Kierkegaard on a theme (prayer) which pushes to the heart of his thought and faith. Perhaps, the best use for this book would be as a spiritual primer for those who wish to move from the portals of prayer into the sanctuary of its meaning and practice.

Lawrence D. Folkemer, Ph.D.
Emeritus Professor of Systematic Theology
Lutheran Theological Seminary
Gettysburg, Pa.

Preface

Soren Kierkegaard's honesty and passion for truth were awesome. These qualities are what make the publication of his prayers today so remarkable. To step into this book of Kierkegaard's prayers, translated by Lois Bowers and edited with comments by Dr. George K. Bowers, is to step inside the soul of Kierkegaard. This father of modern Existentialism is seen here to be honest to God and to himself on a level that may be compared to that of Saint Augustine; his passion for truth is reminiscent of Socrates. Critics who focus on the "irony," "paradox," and "pseudonymous" style of his writing often fail to see it as an instrument of honest self-disclosure. Those who, like his contemporaries, suspect that his use of "many voices" is a form of duplicitous deception do not understand how Kierkegaard is justly credited with giving rise to a multifaceted philosophical movement that has "authenticity" and a higher level of honesty in living as its driving engine.

It becomes clear from these prayers that man needs a higher trans-rational level of communication with God. Kierkegaard is not irrational or anti-reason. Instead he insists that when we talk about God and Divine Revelation the nature of our discourse must be "paradoxical" because of the incapacities of the human mind. Kierkegaard expresses it thus, "We do not begin to comprehend God until we realize that we are comprehended by Him."

In the world of his time, which was well on the way to becoming impersonal and materialistic, Kierkegaard re-discovered the power of commitment or faith. This commitment shines through in his prayers with the realization that words are not enough. We must speak with our lives. The prayers corroborate what he said of all his philosophy, that its purpose is to discover how to become a better Christian.

This translation and publication of Kierkegaard's prayers, hitherto unknown in English, will be a much welcomed addition

11

to the growing body of Kierkegaard literature. Particularly delightful is Dr. George Bowers' step-by-step response to some of Kierkegaard's deep and penetrating insights in the last section of the book. This remarkable work of Dr. Bowers is not the usual thesis and antithesis of the critic but an original, perhaps even a new, literary genre of writing that is more akin to a duet. Bowers moves along with Kierkegaard in a strange and fascinating twosome playing bright, confident, and affirming notes in harmony with Kierkegaard's dark and tantalizing notes of paradox. Dr. Bowers walks with great familiarity and confidence into the dimension of prayer because he himself is a man of prayer. We are grateful that he has given us an inspiring and thoughtful book which both new readers and longtime followers of Kierkegaard will long cherish.

V. Truman Jordahl, Ph.D.
Emeritus Chairman
Department of Philosophy and Religion
Roanoke College, Salem

The Mystique
Of The Pray-er

When a man is as weak and vulner-
able as I am, he will soon learn what
it means to pray.

SK

Introduction

The Mystique Of The Pray-er

A prophet is not without honor, save in his own country. We do not put that assertion in quotes any more because it has become a cliche, used to explain and excuse all manner of the neglect of greatness that occurs in near and unexpected places. In the case of Soren Kierkegaard that place was Denmark.

Kierkegaard was born May 5, 1813, in Copenhagen, the seventh and youngest child of Michael Kierkegaard, who was 56 years old when this son was born. Being the youngest child and also the prodigy of his father's old age, Soren was the favored one of the household and as such was so indulged by his eccentric parent that he never really had to engage in gainful employment for his livelihood. Thus, he gave himself utterly to meditation and writing and to prolonged discussions with anyone willing to endure his sarcasm and satire, anyone willing to be constantly exposed to his biting candor.

Although his first book was published in 1838 and he continued to produce volume after volume until his last entry in his *Journal* in 1853, little note was taken of his writings outside of his home country. Some works were translated into German and later into French. But it was not until the 1940's that any notice was accorded his theology and philosophy in America.

Kierkegaard claimed that he was ignored because he was a Dane. In his *Journal* he declares that had he been born in any other country than Denmark he would have been acclaimed as a genius of the first rank whereas in Copenhagen he was regarded as "a sort of village idiot."

History is replete with instances where great souls have been ignored, and even reviled and persecuted in their own land and in their own time, only to be held in awe and reverence by succeeding generations in other lands — and eventually in their own! Socrates endured such a rejection because it was claimed that his rambling discourses in the marketplace constituted a mortal danger to the youth of Athens. Paul was beaten and jailed more than once in the very cities that were blessed by the churches that he had founded, and eventually he met his death in the very city that became the first center of power and influence for the faith he espoused. Stephen was stoned for his supposed blasphemy and yet he became the lodestar for the very person who consented to his death. And, concerning Jesus, nothing more need be said.

Kierkegaard likened himself to these great heroes of the faith, even to Jesus himself. In his discussion of the three stages of religious experience, his *Concluding Unscientific Postscript*, he states, "While aesthetic existence is essentially enjoyment, and ethical existence essentially struggle and victory, religious existence is essentially suffering."[1] Later, in his confrontation with institutionalized religion, he accepted suffering as an integral part of his identification with the other heroes of the faith.

His disdain for all that worldly pleasures and the joys of the flesh can offer is manifested in his many ways of withdrawing from entangling human relationships and from any inference that worldly pursuits can profit the soul. Yet his sobriquet as Father of Modern Existentialism stemmed, in the most succinct statement of it possible, from his assertion that "only those ideas that can be expressed by being lived can have relevance." He insisted that the "knowing" Ego be distinguished from the "existing" Ego, that man as a thinking being (a gnosiological or epistemological being) must be supplemented by the onto-logical being (man as a living and acting person). In other words, existence involves being and doing as well as thinking. In the scientific world the physicist designates energy as being potential and kinetic, the kinetic energy being not the inert power with possibility, but the moving, working, controlling and controlled power. Philosophically and religiously speaking, mere thought without implementation is not living reality.

16

In practical as well as ideal terms, the bird in the hand is not worth two in the bush because the bird in the hand may be a sick bird or a dead bird, whereas the bird in the bush is a free and living and singing bird, poised to launch out beyond boundless horizons.

Existentially speaking much the same may be said about prayer. One troubled soul, feeling his prayers were ineffectual, writes:

> *My words ascend, my thoughts remain below;*
> *Prayers without thoughts ne'er to heaven go.*

Prayers without actions never reach far, either. Nor do they accomplish anything heavenly for us here or hereafter!

It can be truly affirmed, as one of his biographers observed,[2] that Kierkegaard's life can be described as "cloistered, even for a philosopher." His isolation and insulation from normal interpersonal relationships began early in his childhood. He did not dress as other boys did, nor did he share in their sports and games. His self-effacement he carried to extremes, even recording in his *Journal* a depreciatory description of himself: "Slight, delicate, weak, denied in almost every respect the physical requirements in order to be able to pass for a complete man as compared with others; melancholy, soul-sick, profoundly and absolutely a failure in many ways ..." but then he adds, "one thing was given to me: a pre-eminent intelligence."

Taunted by classmates and other children because of his ungainly appearance, he could not be a "bully" in the usual meaning of the word, but much of his unpopularity with his peers stemmed from the fact that he "bullied" them with his sharp intellect and his cutting wit.

Soren had ambivalent opinions of and feelings for his father. Although his father enforced a strict code of ethics for all members of his family, a rigidity that Soren admired and approved, he was to learn later in life that his father had engaged in illicit relations with the maid of the house before finally marrying her.

Although his father was a melancholy, gloomy, and morose person, he did possess a deep religious fervor. That religious fervor was passed on to the son, but so was the melancholy spirit. Certain passages in his writings may lead the reader to conclude that he was nothing more than a guilt-ridden, distressed, tormented soul who is striving desperately to figure out the meaning of existence and not being very successful at it, for all that. But a deeper probing into his struggles will reveal that he is really one with us all as we individually wrestle with life's deepest issues.

Throughout his childhood he adored his father who was too elderly physically and emotionally to share a youth's desire for companionship in vigorous sports and play. If Soren wanted his dad to go out for a walk or for a game, the answer invariably would be that he was too exhausted. But then, the father would follow with a suggestion that they take a walk in the room without venturing out into the cold. He would take the young lad's hand, and they would walk up and down in one or more of the rooms of the home, all the while pretending that they were walking through the city. During this "inside stroll" the father would point out various imaginary sights and sounds and would describe the buildings and landmarks they were passing, even greeting imaginary passersby and exchanging words with them. The boy would fall into the spirit of the "stroll" and would add remarks and observations of his own to the father's chatter. To the onlooker (had there been any onlooker) it would have appeared to be a strange proceeding, but it did develop the boy's imaginative powers and in a very indirect way sharpened his ability to write effectively in later years.

There were other ways in which the father had tremendous influence on the developing character of the son. From the time when he was a small child, the father helped him build what he called his "gallery of heroes." On the walls of his bedroom Soren had prints of famous men who lived in every age. Again and again his father would come home with such a print to give him and he would accompany the print with some story about the man and what made him great. One day it was Alexander the Great who nearly conquered the then-known world. One day it was the philosopher Socrates who tried to open the minds of his countrymen. One day it was a Man on a cross, being crucified between two common criminals.

Softly, almost tearfully, his father began to tell the boy about this Man who lived as never man had lived, who loved as never man had loved. He told how people had misunderstood Him and because they misunderstood, they took Him out and put Him to death on a cross, which was the way in which every common criminal was made to die in that day.

When the boy heard this, he snatched up the print angrily and hurled it to the floor, exclaiming bitterly, "No common criminal is going to have a place among my gallery of heroes."

Almost sobbing now, the father picked up the precious picture and said, "Not among them, lad, but above them all!" Soren never forgot.

Later, when he came to regard himself as a martyr for the cause of Christ, he wrote, "Already to me as a little child it was made plain as solemnly as possible that the multitude spat upon the very Christ who was truth. This realization is my very life and were I to forget everything else, I would never forget how my Father brought this truth home to me when I was a little child."

In 1840 he became engaged to Regine Olsen, the daughter of a State Councillor. She was an effervescent beauty, always cheerful and affable, much younger than Kierkegaard and a sharp contrast to the gloomy, melancholy man who never appeared to be at ease with either sex. It was a strange relationship, rendered even more incongruous by its sudden termination the very next year for no apparent reason.

Many have concluded that the cause was psychological, the reason being given that his unusual attachment to his father made it impossible for him to relate to normal marital expectations. However, there was a probable deeper religious significance to his rejection of the thought that he could ever find happiness or, more significantly, ever bring happiness to any married relationship with Regine. The discovery of his father's liaison with their house-maid made him conscious of his own guilt before God, both of which he felt that he would have to confess to Regine since to him marriage involved all honesty and frankness.

James Collins has written, "Doubtless, there is room for legitimate psychiatric study of many features of Kierkegaard's character: his relation to his father, his sickliness and melancholy, his unhappy love affair and general attitude toward women and marriage, his inability to communicate with others in a frank and easy way, his extreme sensitivity, and his intensely introspective bent. But psychiatric and psychoanalytic findings cannot rule upon the truth or falsity of his position. It is sheer nonsense to offer as philosophically conclusive the Freudian report that, at his death, Kierkegaard appears to be no more than a 'poor, emaciated, thin schizoid.' "[3]

By strange coincidence the death of Kierkegaard's father paved the way for his open break with the Church and with institutionalized religion. The Lutheran Church was the Established or State Church of Denmark, the members of the clergy being civil servants appointed and paid by the State. This meant security for the priests and the kind of protection afforded such civil servants, but it also meant control by the State and subsequent limitations on the clergy. Kierkegaard resented both the control and the security. He incurred the wrath of fellow seminary graduates by saying soon after he left seminary that all the young would-be priests of the Church were "seeking," but they were not seekers after truth and God; they were seeking comfortable and secure places as ministers of the Church.

To him the very idea of security was contrary to all New Testament Christianity. He even went so far as to say, "To be Christian is one of the most terrible of all torments; it is — and it must be — to have one's hell here on earth."

He concluded that the Holy Spirit was not only being stifled but also being thwarted in the Spirit's attempt to empower the Church. Few men or women possess the humility to sublimate the sense of power that comes from an elevated position. Arrogance is inherent in organization. It is not surprising, then, that a mood, even an attitude, of cynicism should overwhelm one who was as jealous for the honor and integrity of the Church as was Kierkegaard.

He would not accept the appointment as priest of a congregation. He was infuriated when, after inheriting the family estate upon his father's death, it was suggested that since he was now a wealthy man, he could obtain appointment as the priest of some prestigious church. This, he contended, was the Church's obsequious manner of doing business.

Bishop-Primate of the Danish Church was Jacob Peter Mynster, who was the Kierkegaard family priest and who confirmed Soren himself. Since he was his father's favorite priest, Soren did not openly criticize Mynster's theology and practice although he abhorred it. The Bishop enjoyed a privileged and highly remunerative standing as an official of the State, enabling him to live in luxury and to command honor and recognition wherever he went. This was in stark contrast to disciples of the New Testament who were urged by the Master to surrender every notion of material profit or worldly acclaim but rather, were to suffer hatred, persecution and abuse for their faith.

By becoming an "established" institution, with all kinds of regulations and observances like so much entangling undergrowth springing out of worldly plantings, the Church was admitting its spiritual bankruptcy. It had become a "secular institution with a Cultus Minister in the cabinet, enormous property holdings and a large bureaucracy of functionaires and priests. As such, the Church had become a mockery of its origins in the New Testament."

Kierkegaard held to the primacy of the individual. "Eternal verities are not true unless they are true for *me!*" One has no need to subscribe to or obey rules, regulations, and teachings that are articulated and ordained by the Church if they are contrary to the New Testament. He thundered, "Fixed

21

ideas are like a cramp in your foot: the best remedy is to stomp on them." His stomping not only shook the Church, it rattled the theological and philosophical skylights of Denmark and continues to reverberate in the academic and religious world.

Kierkegaard held to the basic doctrines of Lutheranism, the denomination in which he had been reared and the State religion. These included belief in the total depravity of man, original sin, and the sinner's sole trust in deliverance by means of the love and mercy of God through Christ who bore our sins in his own Body on the Tree. As did Luther, he rebelled against the subordination of holy values to secular interests. The goal for himself that he envisioned was much the same as Luther's: "The re-introduction of Christianity into Christendom."

At the funeral of Bishop-Primate Mynster in 1854 Hans Lessen Martensen, who had succeeded Mynster, preached the funeral sermon and extolled the late bishop as a true and faithful apostle of the holy Christian faith after the manner of the apostle Paul. This aroused anew the hostility of Kierkegaard and he attacked both Martensen and Mynster as being the exact opposite of what the New Testament set forth as Christian apostleship.

Works that poured forth from his pen included *Training in Christianity, For Self-Examination, The Established, This Must be Said, So Let it Now Be Said, The Unchangeableness of God, Judgment on Official Christianity.* He also produced articles for *Fatherland,* and even published his own paper, *The Instant.*

His opposition to the established Church, together with another personal vendetta that he had had with *Corsair,* a notorious and widely-read scandal sheet, made him anathema to the religious order. Some even expressed the opinion that he should be banished from the Church. Before any such action could be taken, he announced his own self-imposed excommunication, saying, "The official worship of God (with its claim to being the Christianity of the New Testament) is,

Christianly, a counterfeit, a forgery. So I repeat. This has to be said: by ceasing to take part in the official worship of God as it now is (if in fact you do take part in it) you have one guilt the less, and that is a great one: you do not participate in treating God as a fool.''

He referred to himself as a "dead man" adding that Denmark had need of a dead man. He was willing to consent to his own death, even while he lived, in order to seek to alter the existing order of things. In every age there is need for those who are courageous enough and self-sacrificing enough to oppose the established order in any realm if there is need to follow a nobler and a higher way. Witness one modern theologian's summation of the morbidity and sterility of current Christianity when he said, "The chief trouble with Christians nowadays is that no one wants to kill them any more!"

Under ordinary circumstances you need to understand a man's theology in order to understand his personal religion and his prayer-life. With Kierkegaard to understand his prayer-life is to understand his theology. Therein you find the true nature of the man, stripped of all pretense and pride, something which is not the case when he is confronted by his fellowman. In the presence of other people Kierkegaard felt inferior, persecuted, misunderstood, abused; so that before man he arrogantly sought to defend himself, asserted his superiority, and even struck back. Before God he was humble, penitent, devastated by his guilt and sinfulness and begging for inner peace.

Deluged by his prolific and inordinate flood of criticisms of the Established Church and his acrimonious polemics against his personal adversaries, one scarcely expects to find, perhaps the most overlooked and yet the most precious of his outpourings of the soul, his prayers. As Thomas Gray stated many years ago:

> Full many a gem of purest ray serene
> The dark unfathomed caves of ocean bear:
> Full many a flower is born to blush unseen,
> And waste its sweetness on the desert air.[4]

Such hidden treasure are his prayers, revealing the enraptured depths of his authentic spiritual yearnings and the lofty heights to which the soul can often ascend.

Even in translation these prayers still retain the white glowing fervor of consecration and the vivid vitality of relevance.

How could one so coldly aloof and so uncongenial toward, and suspicious of, his fellowman maintain such an intimate and trusting relationship with God? How could he, having been long under the domination of a materialistic, harsh, and gloomy earthly father, enter into such warm and loving and rewarding communion with the Heavenly Father? Kierkegaard's answer, revealed in the Epilogue to his treatise on *Prayers and Fragments on Prayer,* is irritating to some, irreverent to others, but to him, irrefutable. To him prayer was the true "War of the Worlds," but in his view the "worlds" were earth and heaven, the combatants man and God! By means of prayer we do not win out over God. In prayer God conquers our minds and our attitudes and vanquishes our rebel, errant ways. God's victory over us in prayer gives us the victory over life!

Chapters 1-10 of this text are the translation from the French Tisseau of *Prieres et Fragments Sur la Priere,* published in 1938. Chapters 11-14 contain prayers by the Editor that have been inspired by the philosophical and religious works of Kierkegaard.

How grateful I am to my wife for her patient and painstaking labors in translating this work! How more grateful I am for how graciously she has tolerated the editor as he prayerfully fashioned the final text!

George K. Bowers

---

1. *Concluding Unscientific Postscript,* 236.

2. Josiah Thompson, in introduction to his *Kierkegaard.*

3. *The Mind of Kierkegaard*, pages 18, 19.

4. From Thomas Gray's "Elegy Written in a Country Churchyard."

The Mystique Of Prayer

Prayer is the soul's sincere desire,
Uttered or unexpressed;
The motion of a hidden fire
That trembles in the breast.
— James Montgomery

(The text of *Prayers and Fragments on Prayer,* by Soren Kierkegaard, translated by Lois Bowers)

How presumptuous of us to appear before the throne of grace, O God, even though it is grace sufficient for all our sins. It is not in defiance of Thee that we come, nor do we come in defense of what we have been and what we have done. Since no proper sense of shame has kept us from committing our sins, let now no false sense of shame keep us from confessing our sins. For by laying bare our souls before Thee, we seal the bonds of trust that bind us to Thee.

There is in life one blessed joy, to follow Christ even unto death; and in death one last blessed joy, to follow Christ to life!

SK

(The original of this work of Kierkegaard was not divided into chapters. I have created the divisions for the benefit of the reader. The prayers have been grouped according to the concerns expressed in each brief chapter heading. GKB)

Chapter 1

To My Second,
My Heavenly Father!

As I return thanks to You, O Heavenly Father, for having guarded me here in this life when I needed an earthly father, my further hope and prayer is that You will have more joy in being my Father for the second time than You had this first time around!

*   *   *   *   *

Heavenly Father, our thoughts and our hearts turn to You as we seek You in this hour, not with the indecisive walk of a misguided traveler, but with the sure and certain flight of the bird which knows that it is in familiar territory. Be willing, then, that our confidence in You, which is often fleeting, be not the beguiling appeasement of the fleshly heart; be willing that our aspirations to share Your Kingdom and our hopes to share Your glory be not still-born or clouds without water. From the fulness of our hearts we turn to You, that You may touch our lips with the beauty of the rose as they speak Your praises and that You may feed our hungering souls with the food and drink of Your celestial manna!

*   *   *   *   *

Father, be ever near us with Your mighty power, in order that we may feel that power and all the time and everywhere have the heartfelt assurance that our life, our movements, and our very being are in You!

*   *   *   *   *

29

Father in heaven, be willing that our discourse be not as the flower which opens today and which tomorrow will be thrown into the fire; be willing that it be not as the flower, even though that flower surpasses in magnificence the glory of Solomon. Even though we ignore the marvels of knowledge You have bestowed upon us and allow to fade completely the vigor of mind and spirit that You so graciously have made ours and have looked the other way as we allowed our sensitivities to be lulled to sleep; even though all else be forgotten, never will we forget this: we are saved through Your Son!

* * * * *

Heavenly Father, awaken in us our conscience and teach us to lend our spirit's ear to Your voice, to attend unto Your Word, in order that we may perceive Your will in its pure clarity and glowing splendor as it is in heaven, cleansed from our false terrestrial wisdom and out of reach of the seductive call of our own passions. Teach us to be vigilant, albeit with fear and trembling, and be willing, when the Law speaks most insistently and when its gravity fills us with fright, when the thunder rolls from Mt. Sinai — oh, be willing that we may hear, above the noise of the thunder and the pulsing beat of our own fear, that louder, clearer Still Small Voice, reminding us that we are Your children. So shall we cry with joy, "Abba, Father."

* * * * *

Christ walked on the waters. Father, calm the waves that buffet our minds; still the tempests that rage in our hearts. Be still, my soul, so that the Divine may stir in thee. Be still, my soul, so that God may repose in thee and that His peace may cover you with its shade. How often we have proved that the world can not give us peace! How often we have acknowledged that You alone can give it, for that is your promise to us! Even as the world can not give us peace, so the world cannot rob us of the peace that You give!

* * * * *

When thoughts of You, our Father, awaken in our souls, grant that such thoughts are not aroused as the bird which is frightened and confused, and so flutters about without any sense of direction, but as an infant who awakens from sleep with a divine smile, knowing it is cradled in Your Everlasting Arms!

* * * * *

Father in Heaven, walk with us in close companionship as You walked with Your people, the Jews, long ago. Prevent our believing that we can ever be emancipated from Your company. Help us instead to dwell and grow in the sacred milieu of Your love as seed grows in the salubrious enfoldment of land and sky. Prevent us from turning in disbelief from Your assurances and when success comes our way, remind us that without Your help we can do nothing, we can be nothing.

* * * * *

Father! Make our heart Thy temple where Thou canst dwell in honor and in splendor. Even as the Philistine idol Dagon was shattered and lay in fragments at the conqueror's feet, so may every impure thought, every earthly desire, be shattered and laid before those Pierced Feet of Him Who died that we might be dead to sin and alive evermore to God!

* * * * *

Heavenly Father, open the fountains of our eyes that a torrent of tears, like a deluge, may pour forth and efface the spiritual debris of our past which has not found grace in Your eyes. Give us a sign as of old, when You sent the Rainbow as a merciful and inviting Doorway back into Your favor. Never allow sin such power over us as to make it necessary for You to rescind Your promise and visit our world again with Your judgment.

* * * * *

O Father Celestial! Teach us to walk as ever in Thy presence. May our thoughts and our acts be not as strangers come from afar to pay rare visits in Your domain, but as natives proving that we live in You and You in us. Of what use could it be to us that our faces shine as did Moses' face when he communed with You if, as Moses did, we turn our face from You? At times I feel abandoned, far away in my isolation as was the tax collector in former days so that I can only turn my face toward You. Do not let me turn completely away as did he who put his hand to the plow and thus worked his way out of Your favor. Though valley and mountain and sea stretch out before me and overwhelm me with their vastness, though a paralyzing sense of insignificance envelopes all my days, renew that deathless promise that whoever is smallest in Your Kingdom is greater than any outside that Kingdom.

*　*　*　*　*

God in the Heavens, let me feel my worthlessness, not to *despair* at my wretched state but to be *aware* of the grandeur of Your bounty. This desire is not, as the jester in me would say, like the attitude of the glutton who fasts in order that he may indulge his greed at the feast. It is, rather, to partake of Your goodness, Your mercy, and Your love in the realization that with that as our fare we need never hunger or thirst again.

*　*　*　*　*

Chapter 2

Turn Not Away From Me, Even Though I Turn Away From You!

Turn not Your face from me, O Father; make it shine anew so that I can walk in Your company and not stray where Your Voice (which should be heard always and everywhere) is no longer audible to me. Make me to listen with heart as well as with ear, even though Your Voice strikes fear in me because of my sick and sin-stained spirit. My sins and waywardness shut me off from You and from my fellowman so that I am lost — yes, lost! But Thou, O Lord Jesus Christ, came to seek and to save the lost. You left the ninety-and-nine and searched for the straying lamb until You found it and brought it home to the fold. And I? — You know where I am hiding — and why! Come, if only within hearing distance, my Lord, and only speak and I will obey. As I stumble warily back into our Father's presence, be my intercessor, O Holy Spirit, and pray for me as did Abraham for corrupt Sodom. Since the dying tree ofttimes can be revived if one live branch remains, probe deeply into my heart and see if there be but one groping outreach toward true godliness. Let there be no parting of Vine and branches, O Divine Redeemer, but such a trust and reliance on God's sustenance and support as shall bring healing and new life. And with the restored fruitfulness that new life brings, may I not forget as did the nine healed leapers, but move my heart and my feet to hurry back to Your throne of grace, praising and thanking You for that newness of life into which I have risen from the grave of lostness, quick and eager to be Your servant forever!

*   *   *   *   *

It is from Your Hand, Heavenly Father, that we receive all that we need. Sages and pundits the world over bewail those needs unmet and those hungers unfulfilled. We know, because we understand Your compassionate love, that You only withhold the boon, which we importune and earnestly plead for, in order to bestow an abundance greater than we can ever ask or think.

* * * * *

O Lord our God, not only do You *know* our sorrow better than do we ourselves, but You *feel* it, too. You understand the burden, the heavy grief that we bear. Make us humble in our rebellion against life's injustices so that we do not turn for comfort to those who are like wandering stars to whom is reserved the blackness of the darkness forever, or to those who are like the raging waves of the sea foaming out their own shame. You are our refuge and our strength, and there is none other.

* * * * *

In the midst of life's storm and strife, we turn, O God, to You to ask of You that peace that passes understanding. Once it is given, grant us the assurance that nothing can wrest that peace from us — not our evil earthly desires, not our avarice, not the boiling unrest of our hearts — for we recognize these as greater dangers than any foe in this stormy, strife-ridden world around us.

* * * * *

Lord God, every living creature turns its eyes toward You as do all on earth turn toward the sun, seeking nourishment and sustenance. You open Your Hand in compassion and magnanimity so that all may go away filled. Not only do You hear the cry of need from the wild beast, but You bend Your ear to catch the oft-unuttered complaints of man. Lift up the thoughts of those to whom You have given much, that they may set their affection on things that are above and seek heavenly treasures. So shall they know that every good and perfect gift is from above and comes down from the Father Who sheds His light on our path, and that only what You give can ever satisfy. Teach those to whom You have given little that nothing is so modest that it will not be, with Your blessing, good measure, pressed down, and shaken together, and running over!

* * * * *

O Lord my God, give me the courage to hope. O God of pity, allow my soul to never become withered and sterile so that I no longer reach out in glorious expectation. When I am tempted to feel that You no longer listen to my raucous complaints or my silent sighs, remind me to continue my insistent praying until, like the bothered judge who was vexed at the importunate widow, You answer out of love and pity.

* * * * *

If, as it is said, earthly love makes one eloquent, how much more does one's love for Thee, O God, bring to these hearts and voices of ours an eloquence to rival that of the Heavenly Chorus. How proper that such eloquence praises the Very One Who formed these hearts and lips for prayer and praise!

* * * * *

Heavenly Father! Draw our hearts to Thee so that our desire is where our treasure should be. Let not feckless thoughts and yearnings rule our earthly stay, so that when at last You call us and summon us to Your Kingdom that is beyond, our departure from the earth be not a sad separation from a world that has been too much with us, but a joyful reunion with You. We do not know the time or hour; perhaps that is still distant from us. But when death thrusts its will upon us and it seems we are plunged into sombre night, when all our restless desires fade and anxiety increases fears of what lies ahead, then, O God our Father, teach us that we belong to You and Your Kingdom more than we belong to the kingdom of this world or

35

to any power that has sought to rule us in this life. And fortify this firm conviction in our hearts.

*   *   *   *   *

Father Celestial! You loved us first. In a world where we are seduced by false loves and lovers, where restless souls succumb to specious but spurious affection and we are submersed in the agony of the past and the fright of the future and the distress of the present, assure us that we still can love. Remind us that we love because You first loved us; thus, our love can be that pure and holy affection, which only God and His beloved people can know and show!

*   *   *   *   *

Lord of Compassion! We know that every perfect gift comes from You. You have not sent us into the world empty-handed. Our hands are filled with Your bounty, but let us not therefore clench our fists lest we lose it all. Rather, open our hands and our hearts that we may relay Thy benediction, thus bestowing good and perfect gifts on others when we give!

*   *   *   *   *

Heavenly Father, we know that all research has its promise. How, then, can we not search for Thee, the sole Dispenser and Guarantor of promises? We know, too, that whoever seeks need not go far in his searching for, the more sacred is the thing which he seeks, the nearer it is to him because it is dearer to him. If he seeks for Thee, O God, You are very near because You are very dear. But we know that all research has its disappointments. Should he, therefore, who puts his confidence in Your companionship, shun all risk as the search grows arduous; should he glower and rage at the veiling shadows and the stormy skies rather than probe the gathering darkness for Your kindly Smile; should even the dying one, for whom You are merely changing a life-abode, tremble at the uncharted journey which lies before him as he leaves behind the fears and the miseries of this world; is it puzzling or strange that the wicked and worthless wastrel wonders how he can presume to seek Thee, too? He seeks Thee by confessing his sins and his unworthiness to be blessed by any discovery. He finds Thee in Thy forgiveness!

* * * * *

Inquiringly, to You, Father Celestial, we turn our attention and our desire for Your attention, for You are the One Who approves or disapproves; You are the One who lifts up or puts down. The world gives us its approval and exalts us among our fellowmen, placing us in positions of import and power, bestowing upon us high honors and great expectations. In Your sight, however, there is displeasure with what we do, what we are, what we become. Of what joy or profit is it to win glory from sinful man if we arouse only displeasure and disdain from our Holy God? Of what blessing and joy can there be in earthly achievements when there is failure in fulfilling Divine expectations? Befriended by man, we languish as strangers in the sight of our Lord. No proper sense of shame has kept us from committing our sins; now let no false sense of shame keep us from confessing our sins. Our Just and Holy God, we shift the orientation of our very being away from the sinful pathways of this world and swing full-circle in our resolution to conform to Your Word and Your Will. Henceforth we will cherish what You approve; henceforth will we shun what You disapprove. Thus, You Who can readily put down will speedily lift us up, O Father, our Father Who art in heaven.

* * * * *

Father Celestial, to Whom belong boundless wisdom and deepest compassion, You understand us, our goings out and our comings in; You know what is in man. But You desire that we understand You. Even as our Master answered not a word to his raucous accusers, thus exposing their fraudulent deceit and revealing his own innocence, so You speak

37

in love and understanding when You speak not a word! For one is speaking when he remains silent in order to show the listener that he is beloved. One is speaking when, as teacher, he listens to the pupil. One is speaking when he demonstrates that profound understanding comes from listening. Man may fear that he is lost in the desert of abandonment when he does not hear Your Voice. But it is only the Golden Moment of stillness in the intimacy of conversation and communion. When we come imploring, pleading, promising, even threatening, and You greet us with nary a word, You understand us completely and You speak by answering our needs. Bless, then, the Golden Moment of silence, for the same Paternal Love is ours when You are silent as well as when You speak!

* * * * *

Chapter 3

You Support The Worlds, Our Father; Support Me!

Heavenly Father, great and boundless is the expanse of Your Kingdom. You support the constellations and the pillars of a widening universe; You bear up the weight of a weary world; and You direct the tiniest footstep on the pathways of earth. The grains of sand along the ocean's shore do not approach in number the sum of all the responsibilities that are Yours. In spite of Your boundless power and limitless sovereignty You give heed to all those who have received and continue to receive from You life and being. Especially do You give heed to lowly man whom You have formed by Your Word. You bend down to listen to each one so attentively and so caringly that, amidst all the cacophony and confusion of the daily clamor, each person is assured that You are giving all concern to him alone. Not only do You pay heed to the one who commands and leads; not only do you listen to the voice of him who prays in intercession for loved ones as if he had a special conduit to Your favor. No! You pay heed also to the man who is the most miserable, the most abandoned, the most solitary — whether he moves among the multitude or plods along in the trackless desert. And if others have forgotten him and cast him out of their caring; if in the crowd he has lost all identity; if he has ceased, really, to be a human being and has become no more than a number on a list; You know him, O God; You have not forgotten him. Wherever he is, lost in the desert or just as lost and unnoticed in the crowd; whatever state he is in, whether it be in agonizing pain, or in bondage to terrible and terrifying thoughts, abandoned of men, so cut off from communication that in the prolonged silence he has forgotten his native tongue — nevertheless You, O God, have not forgotten him and You hear and comprehend his speechless speech! You know at once how to find the road that leads to him, and rapid as sound and prompt as light You speed to his side. If it seems that You are late in reaching him, it is not because You are penurious or uncaring so that You are withholding the fulness of Your response and denying the fulfillment of his deep, deep need. It is, rather, because You are aware of the need for a proper place and a propitious time, where and when Your blessing will be most precious. Lord, our God! In the day of his distress man cries to You for Your help and deliverance. In the days of his peace and joy he cries to You in thanksgiving. How very joyous it is to give thanks when into our lives You have poured down from above every good and perfect gift. But there comes a deeper joy and peace when man can give thanks in the midst of his misfortune, his abandonment, his hopelessness — when it seems that his own thoughts have betrayed him, when all reason has left him, when there is only discouragement and disillusionment. Ah, to give thanks then! That is to really show the depth of our devotion, to *love God* when the world *hates us!* When the odds are all against us, when there are those who would seek to convince us that we are without hope and without God in our world, then need we more than ever to hold on to Him Who holds fast to us, Lord, You know all things and, no matter what those "all things" may bring us, You know that we love You. Whether life gives or takes away, we know that You love us!

*   *   *   *   *

Preserve me from becoming a fool who resents the chastisement and punishment with which You meet his wrongdoing, or the fool who suffers and chafes at his punishment, but denies that You have any sovereignty over it or over him. Preserve

40

me from becoming the fool who refuses to accept divine favor and favors, or the recalcitrant fool who gains life's blessings to his eternal loss because he denies that they ever come from Thee!

* * * * *

Celestial Father, as the earthly father lets go of a son that the boy may make his way in some strange far country, so You have released Your hold on questing humanity that men might make their way in this strange and unfamiliar world. No more can man see You face-to-face. No more can he listen with fleshly ear to Your guiding Voice. Although the open road is now before him, he finds himself a prisoner in the world. He will become discouraged and impatient with the slow and stumbling pace of achievement and success. Give him firm courage when he discovers that wrong paths are readily available and easy to follow, whereas strait is the gate and narrow the way that leads aright. The stars in the heavens will often appear to be his foes; events may well prove overpowering; human misery will assail at every turn; and even the elements will conspire to overthrow him. Why, as a Father, send You us into such a world? In that long-ago Far Country the Prodigal Son learned, too, the hard facts about being deprived of the love of home. He had the courage to persevere in a land without love. Things had changed at home. People had changed; the elder brother was no longer a loving and proud sibling but resentful and hostile. No doubt the servants resented preparing for such a wastrel the fatted lamb. But the *father* was still the same; his love never faltered or faded. The returning sinner quickly concludes that he will not be received as was this beloved child who was troublesome and rebellious. The Prodigal could not be sure, either, but he *had faith* that joy and love awaited his return. We, who are dead in sin even while still alive and who are on our way to perdition, believe that the Father of Compassion waits to welcome us at the end of the road to salvation! At last, we are home!

* * * * *

Father Celestial, we know that all the time and everywhere You are a Silent PRESENCE. If man intrudes on Your Presence, crying out from a bed of pain, from bodily misery as profound as the ocean depths or misery even more profound, the depthless misery of his sin, we know that You, in Your Silent Presence, stand near to hear. You are also a Silent Presence in the place of worship where faithful ones assemble, perhaps fleeing from dull thoughts or followed by them. When they leave that place of worship, they still may bear their same heavy burdens, but their hearts are light, for in their weakness You have given strength; in their anxious fear You have given consolation, courage, and contentment, even to the dying one, for Your Silent Presence assures of everlasting life. Please, then, O God, Father of all, that You will be found at this hour, not only in the witness of Your excellent gifts, which we carry away in our hands, but in the perfect trust and reassurance that we bear away in our hearts. Yes, in our human frailty we perceive gradations, setting off joy from sorrow, good from evil, light from darkness. But it is Your good and perfect gift to us to see them all as just another part of the world that You have asked us to overcome!

* * * * *

Father in Heaven, You Who are incomprehensible in the marvels of Your Creation, You dwell in a faraway realm of dazzling splendor which human eye cannot endure. We know You through Your providential love and care but such knowledge is feeble, indeed, and may serve only to veil from our eyes the true brilliance of Your splendor. Yet, You are still more incomprehensible in Your grace and in Your pity. What is man, indeed, that You are mindful of him, You Who are infinite and more? What is the son of a fallen race that you desire to visit you, You the Saint? And what is the sinner, that Your Son desires because of him to come to the world, not to judge but to save? Nor does he make known the place of his sojourn in order that lost man can run back to him, but he looks for the man who is lost and hastens to search out the sinner. He has no lair as do the beasts; he has not even a stone on which he can lay his head. Willingly he hungers in the desert and thirsts upon the Cross. Saviour, Father of Compassion! What can one do in response to the blessings of such sacrifice? Man cannot even give thanks unless the Spirit of the living God stirs up thanksgiving in him. Teach us recognition of our sinful helplessness that, like the broken heart, gasping under the weight of his wickedness, who says in his sadness: "It is impossible that God can have compassion thus," — or like the one who, accepts in faith the blessed assurance, says in his joy: "It is impossible." Or like the one, whom death appears to separate from loved ones, but who discovers to his glad surprise that there is that promised reunion beyond, can only cry at the moment of that reunion: "It is impossible!" Heavenly Father, even though man has heard this joyous message of Thy compassion from tenderest infancy, it is not for all that less incomprehensible, nor for all that, even though he meditate and speculate day and night, the wonder of it is undiminished.

* * * * *

Chapter 4

Sometimes You Are A Puzzle To Me; Let Me Not Be A Puzzle To You.

The enigma of Thy grace, like the enigma of man himself, is like the treasured affection of lovers, incomprehensible at first, but unveiling its priceless wonder as time goes by. O the indolence of man's discernment! O mistaken wisdom of this world! O tarnished blemish of slumbering faith! O miserable forgetfulness of the cold heart! Deliver us, O Savior, from them all and to the humble believer grant the wisdom to discern the beautiful, the good the true. Oh, deliver us from evil!

* * * * *

Father in Heaven, all of us are guilty at times of speaking one way about a person when he is present and in an entirely different way when he is absent; what we say and the way we say it depends on whether we are talking *to* the man when he is with us or whether we are talking *about* him when he is not. But of Thee, O God — how would we be able to speak of Thee in Thy absence when Thou art everywhere! How would we be able to vacillate from this to that when Thou art ever the same! O God, to guide the meditation of our soul, its edification, its discipline, and its purification, send Thy Spirit to assure us that Thou art ever with us!

* * * * *

Father in Heaven, do not be with our sins against us, but be with us against our sins, so that each thought of You, when it awakens in the soul, may enable us to remember, not our transgressions, but Your pardon, and also to remember, not the devious way in which we wandered away and were lost, but the merciful way in which You found us and saved us by Your grace!

* * * * *

Heavenly Father, exercise Your inexhaustible patience with us, Your children. We are often forward in our actions, bringing misery upon ourselves, and we are often fractious in our speech, bringing misery to others. When, as mischievous and mistaken children we seek to remedy the damage from our obtuse perversity, we invoke Your help. Since we believe that You are our Father and we are spiritual infants, receive us as Your legitimate children and not as the animal that feigns to be the offspring of its Master. Exercise Your Paternal Patience with us, our Father, and guide us to use, not the language of the perverse infant, but the language You have taught us!

* * * * *

Our relationship with Thee, O God, is not as that with a person from whom we buy. Of necessity (and desire!) it is You Who gives first, and those gifts are faith, hope, love, the aspirations after the good and propitious opportunities — all without money and without price. You give all for nothing. The lowly pagan thinks, since his gods will give nothing for nothing, that You make exorbitant demands for Your gifts. If You dealt thus with Your people, You would be descending to man's level and would no longer be God, for God calls us up to his level. As earthly parents, we give to our children, and often, with proud generosity, they will return a portion of that gift to us, really giving us what already belonged to us. We do not, for that reason, reject their gifts or the givers but love them more. It is like the parent aiding his child in writing a greeting to the parent himself, who receives it as the child's own. The error of the pagan is that he knows *about* his god, that he is not a free giver; however the believer *knows* his God and that His blessings are a free gift!

* * * * *

46

O God, there are in the world around us so many things which seek to turn us away from You. That is why we repair to Your House where, to be sure, there reigns an atmosphere capable of deceiving us, as if all danger and fear were removed since we are in this place. But here is where we must avoid the supreme danger, the danger of sin, and the even greater danger of ignoring the suffering and death of Christ that delivers us from sin!

* * * * *

Lord Jesus Christ, many, many things seek to divert us and to attract us and to direct us to the empty and the useless. Each offers some special attention, its own special allurement. But You are the eternal Strong One. Draw us, then, by Your mighty power to Your side. We call You our Redeemer, for You have come to the world to break the bonds of vain care and the heavy chains of sin with which we have enslaved ourselves. We call You Saviour, for You do save us in liberating us from these shackles, which we cannot see but keenly feel. It was God's will, His very intent, from the foundations of the world, that You render possible and consummate our sanctification. For that reason alone You did descend the lowest in order to draw us to the highest. You accepted our lowly state in this fallen world in order to raise us to our true abode.

* * * * *

Father Celestial! In the world around us one person is stronger, another is weaker; the first becomes very proud of his strength, the second sighs and perhaps knows, alas, jealousy. But in ourselves we are all feeble before Your face, You the Powerful, You the only Strong!

* * * * *

Father Celestial! In the world around us one person is stronger, another is weaker; the first exhausts all his power to puff himself up; the second rails and scoffs at all powers except his own. But in Your sight our would-be strengths

47

are weakness and our weaknesses are strength when we are ruled by You, the All-Powerful, the Matchless Strength!

* * * * *

Heavenly Father, how often the congregation directs its prayers to You for all those who are sick and afflicted. When any one is touched by a mortal malady and is in the last extremity, he very often requests the special prayers of the congregation. May each one of us make certain that he recognizes which malady is the fatal malady; and may he realize when he is touched by it, for it is a malady that afflicts us all. And You, Jesus Christ, our Saviour, Who has come into the world to heal those who suffer from this malady (and all of us do!), but of whom You can heal only those who know they are touched by it, guide us in our sinning to take swift recourse to You for healing. And You, O Holy Spirit, imbue us with the eager spirit to *be* healed. Be present with us every moment lest in our agony of soul we seek to hide both self and sin from the sight of man and from the touch of our God. Nor allow us to absent ourselves from the Great Physician, for in His presence is our healing.

* * * * *

You alone, O God, can stir up my spirit. All the while that I think on You, my whole being bows at Your footstool as Your obedient slave. Although to man my powers and my abilities seem great, in Your sight they are nothing. In either case, whether impressive to humanity but insignificant to the Divine, they are gifts and powers that You have given. When I think on Your sufferings, my Lord and my Saviour, I cannot use my place of privilege in the pulpit as a platform for complaint, but by Your leave I continue to serve and by Your power I continue to thrive.

* * * * *

God of love, You have commanded us to pardon our enemies, our brothers in error, not seven times, but seventy times seven. When, then, would You permit Yourself to withhold pardon from the worst sinner if he repents?

* * * * *

You Who are present everywhere, even when I merely *think* of what I want to say and how to say it, You know immediately what I am thinking before I even speak! When I resolve to come to Your house, You are there awaiting my arrival. Strengthen, then, in us this firm assurance of Your presence everywhere at every hour.

* * * * *

We wish to receive all things from Your Hand. If it is a matter of glory and honor, we wish to receive them from Your Hand; if it is a matter of raillery and insult, we wish to receive them from Your Hand. O may we receive both the one and the other with the same great joy and recognition, for there is scarce any difference between them. For us there is none at all if it is our indubious affirmation that they all come from You!

* * * * *

Father Celestial! In the night, when we prepare for sleep, we find our consolation in the thought that You are He Who watches over us, and when in the morning we awaken and even all through our waking day, if we could not trust that He who never slumbers nor sleeps but keeps the nighttime watch, is not our daytime Guide and Keeper, what desolation! The difference that we establish between sleeping and waking is only a whimsical distinction, as if we needed You to watch over us as we sleep, whereas we can guard and keep ourselves when we are awake.

* * * * *

Heavenly Father, You Who care for the sparrow without cruelly demanding that it be as You but on the contrary, in Your love You put Yourself in its place with paternal solicitude, just so do You care for man. If You demand that man resemble You, a demand that You do not exact from the sparrow, it is not a cruel and unreasonable expectation. No, in Your paternal solicitude You put Yourself in man's place, and

49

You are Yourself the One Who gives him strength to fulfil Your demand and expectation.

* * * * *

Men, we carry the Sacred Thing in a fragile earthly vase. But You, Holy Spirit, when You live in man, You live in that which is infinitely less! You, the spirit of holiness, You live in impurity and contamination. You, the spirit of wisdom, You live in folly. You, the spirit of truth, You live with him who has deceived himself. Although we are all of these, O continue to stay. O Creator and Renewer, You do not seek Your ease, a vain search by making Yourself Your dwelling. O continue to stay, in order that one day You may consummate Your joy in a dwelling that You have Yourself prepared in my defiled and foolish and deceiving heart!

* * * * *

Teach me, O God, not to torture myself and not to make a martyr of myself in suffocating reflection, but to take deep and wholesome breaths of faith!

* * * * *

Chapter 5

We Confess, Our Savior, Not So That You Will Know Us Better But That We Will Know Ourselves Better!

Saviour, Jesus Christ, may You fill my thoughts in such a way that even by looking on me one can see that my thoughts are of You. And how would one see it? Would it be because I am gazing skyward? That might signify that I am looking at the stars or even at some figment of the imagination. No, if by Your example You would give me the conviction that though I am modest, scorned and ridiculed, I still proclaim Your doctrine, then one would be able to see in my person (not in my appearance but in my daily being) that I have thought of You. And you, powerful celestial ones, you celestial legions that uphold the good, aid in augmenting my voice in order that it be, if possible, heard by all the world. I have only one word to say; but if the power were given me to express one lone word, one lone phrase, in such a way that it would remain forever fixed and unforgettable — my choice has been made. I have this word; I would say: our Saviour Jesus Christ! You, O Christian, need remember nothing else.

* * * * *

The sigh of a suppliant! — Father of love, I have succeeded in nothing save in knowing that You are love. And still, I have not succeeded in maintaining that You are love. No matter where I turn, I am unable to evade or avoid the truth that You are love. Although I fail, I believe that, through Your love, You allow that failure. O Love Infinite!

* * * * *

51

O You, my Saviour and my Lord, You Who were and are love and Who through love came into the world to suffer and die before our very eyes without ceasing to love, You brought unhappiness to Your first followers. For every one of them there was at first no firm assurance of the joy and serenity of a peaceful life; they had to flee in fright and in terror. For Your Mother, You were a sword through the heart; for Your disciples, You were an occasion of scandal; the entire world rose up to make charges against You, that You brought misfortune to all people. You Who were "Love" and Who had come, through love, to save us all, why did You not humiliate and embarrass those who were Your foes? Then there would not have come to my mind any question about putting down those who put You down. Consequently, when I despair and am tempted to humiliate and embarrass others, I am in agony at thoughts of You and Your anger at me, You Who humiliated none but persisted in love. Oh, feeble, indeed, is the constraint that tempers us poor humans as over against that Perfect Love of Yours, which is divine!

* * * * *

You Who in our infancy received our vow, You to Whom at baptism we promised our fidelity, Father Celestial, may we throughout our life never forget our promise or our betrothing, so that we forget to come to Your Marriage Feast. Whatever excuses we make are pretexts and lack significance. The only credible excuse would be if we were to lack an invitation!

* * * * *

A sigh of anguish in the battle that overwhelms my strength: O God, my God, even in the midst of insignificant things You bear down on me with all Your weight. In the least move that I make, I commit a colossal mistake, a grievous sin that merits the severest punishment, and I fall under the weight of Your judgment. No, I do not have the strength to bear up You Whom I have let down. Let me tell you: you are as much in error as the man who concludes that he is blind, only because he has extinguished the divine light within him. On the contrary, it is God Who desires to bear you up and to do it with as much ease as it would be with difficulty if you sought to do it on your own.

*   *   *   *   *

To God: on those occasions when I have been able to understand Your bounty toward me, I have been, as far as is humanly possible, recognizant of each blessing granted. O God, in the relationship between man and the Divine, it is not necessary to comprehend all Your ways in order to conclude that You are good. Help me to be thankful also even when I do not comprehend. In childlike naivete I could pretend that I understand and have concluded that You are less than charitable. Abominable thought! — for should I do so, I would bring eternal sorrow and misery upon myself. It often seems to me that my relationship with God is like that which I would have with an inquisitor: it would be necessary for me to bring into play all my reason and all my powers. In such circumstances I could never be sure whether I have laid hold on the truth or if I have deceived myself. You have said simply: yes, in this conclusion you have erred. You have acted contrary to the truth; consequently, you are at fault. O my God, there is communion between man and his Maker. No, God be praised we do not come face-to-face as equals. No, even when I am in error, it is Your providence that takes over immediately in spite of my waywardness and weaves even my error into Your Grand Design, in Your love cancelling out the millions of consequences of my error and making even my error profitable to me.

For a time Your help enabled me to succeed in everything I did, but then, there came a time when it appeared that You were denying me success in anything. My interpretation was that You had utterly forsaken me, that You desired no longer to continue with me. I thought it was my bounden duty to thank You for the good fortune and happiness You brought me, but there was no awareness of Your present Help and Your helpful Presence in my failures. O smallness of my heart, to think in such a small way of You! No, Your design for me is that I move up to higher, better things, to learn thanksgiving and praise even when confronted by unhappiness and misfortune.

* * * * *

There was a time, O God, when I stood in humble awe at the beauty of Your precious gifts. Joy immeasurable was mine. Then all changed: I succeeded in nothing, yet even when fresh defeats and failures came my way, my thoughts were still of You. My joy was greater at every remembrance of Your love, for You need not prove that love by gifts; Your love, which is infinite and everlasting, is beyond proof. Nor do I need the aid of proof to believe and trust Your love, for it is not a theorem in need of demonstration, it is a dictum that requires no proof. Even when my soul wearies of man's idle prattle, Your love is the foundation rock of truth.

* * * * *

In the depths of my soul, O God, You have put the blessed assurance that You are love. You have treated me as does the loving father indulgently treat his child, and again and again I have thus been assured of Your love. But then, when that assurance had left me, I faltered in that at which I had always succeeded and I became confused. Anguish and fear overcame me and I thought the lofty expectations of me were far beyond my powers to fulfill. Then I thought that perhaps I had become too presumptive; I was baffled, concluding that my failure was Your way of chastising me for my presumption. In my concern I said: it is my many errors that have snatched You from me. Miserable ingrate that I was! — as if to conclude that it was my former wisdom and virtues which influenced You to love me, as if there were such vagaries in Your love as to make You change in a moment! O heart full of folly and of vanity, when you erroneously seek to take credit for,

54

of all things, meriting God's love for past achievements, and practice the sweet self-persuasion that you have been worthy of that love! O no, no, God be praised, never has there been the impulse to claim my right to have God's love. Should that be so, man would perish in overwhelming anguish the moment that he ever felt that he was no longer worthy of God's love.

* * * * *

A sigh in the struggle! — O, when all kinds of obstacles stand in my way and one setback follows after another, often bringing more anguish than human strength can bear, one thing remains to console me, O God, and that is the reinforcement of the Spirit. You Who propose and dispose in all things, and in each instance there are millions of possibilities so that when You permit these misfortunes and afflictions to befall me in spite of Your boundless love for me, I can at least know that it is not because of my own shortcomings. You withdraw into the background in order that the Spirit may draw me into closer fellowship with Thee.

If this were not the case, if You were not to permit me to sink to the depths, it would not be possible for me to realize my true plight, my reversals and my need for Your paternal reprimand, which opens my eyes to my lost state and permits the Spirit to lift me up to the lofty stature God plans for me.

* * * * *

You loved us first, O God. Alas, we speak of it as if You loved us first one time only, historically speaking, when in very truth, without ceasing, You love us first many times all day long and all life through! When we awaken in the morning and our souls turn at once toward Thee, You are first; You have already turned toward us. If I rise at dawn and in the very first second of my awakening my soul turns to You in prayer, You have beat me to it; You have already turned in love toward me. Thus, we speak as ingrates if, unthankful and unaware, we speak of You as having loved us first only one time.

* * * * *

Chapter 6

How Thankful We Are
That You Understand
Our Misunderstandings!

Outpouring! O my God, how many times, in recognition of unspeakable joy, have I failed to realize the astonishing manner in which things happen. I have missed the real significance of vastly important events. But many times, too, to my lasting joy, You in Your wisdom, have used even my misjudgments so that, though all might have been lost through my stupidity, You have turned eventualities into blessings.

* * * * *

Heavenly Father! Give us to understand that whatever happens to us comes from You; therefore, since it comes from You, it cannot decrease our powers; no, no, it can only make us more useful.

* * * * *

O my God, my God, unhappy and distressing was my infancy; full of torments was my youth. I lamented, I sighed, I cried. Still, I lift up my voice in thanksgiving to You, not for Your overruling wisdom through it all, but for Your infinite and matchless love. Man can expect a life of thirty, forty, perhaps seventy years. If, from these years of my sojourn I have exacted only the sweets and the tender morsels of life and nothing of the bitter and the evil to remember in the life beyond, in Your gentleness You have reminded me of this very thing, that I ought not to seek to shelter myself from suffering.

Although in love You do protect me in life's adversities, You do make it incumbent upon me to accept a measure of suffering as an integral ingredient in my happiness. For each measure of suffering thus accepted is a beginning of our suffering with You and will to endless ages be an everlastingly precious acquisition. For one remembers forever these sufferings. That may seem strange and, on first sight, even contrary to our Christian belief. But (as Kierkegaard shows in his "The Gospel of Suffering"), the suffering accepted and endured with Christ is a victory of the spirit and the triumph of eternity over time; therefore, it is a wholesome, joyous, invigorating source of eternal blessedness, since it is eternity lived in time. One does not recall suffering itself in the importance which it assumes in time, but in its moral and religious value for eternity. That is why here, as everywhere in my writings, I have urged that suffering be remembered, not for its temporal usefulness or benefit or sorrow, but for its eternal impact.

> *(Immediately after this "outpouring," which introduces a long fragment, Kierkegaard writes: "A pagan* mentions that the greatest voluptuous person of the Orient, Sardanapale, had this inscription carved on his tomb: 'I have brought into my tomb all the joys of the earth,' to which another pagan** would have replied, 'How? You have not even been able to retain one of them during your life!' ")*
> **Cicero, in his "Concerning Ends"*
> ***Aristotle*

No, the joys of this life do not lend themselves to ready recollections in the life to come. If, then, a man were to escape all suffering in this world, what a terrible thing it would be for him to be clothed in fine linens and purple garments — attended by a pasha with seventeen trains of persons with rings in their noses, bearing all the insignia before which every knee would bow — what a terrible thing to be bereft of all that which has made him a part of suffering humanity and thus have nothing to remember through all eternity!

*   *   *   *   *

You Who have come into the world for the express purpose of suffering, and Who have borne the most onerous burden of suffering, made even more onerous by the added weight of sorrows, from Your very first breath in this earthly life You knew in advance and freely accepted all that lay before You. Nor, although You had the power to do so, did You evade it. All Your earthly stay has been a life of suffering, culminating in an ignominious death. Thanks to You for having, to our lasting joy, sanctified suffering by Your deportment and demeanor, bringing the brilliant dawn of comprehension to us when suffering has long kept us in a protracted night of ignorance and confusion. Thanks to You that man can never ignore the great blessing bestowed upon him in suffering, giving him such great consolation and reinforcement through this divine revelation. Never may he have the temerity to disregard the diversity in our sufferings, Your innocence for man's guilt, Your humility for his pride, Your death which brings to him life forever.

* * * * *

Yes, O God our Lord, it is true that we are often overcome with a weary apathy. When Your blessings inundate me, I want to assemble all my powers of gratitude and praise to thank You, but, alas, I find myself distracted, for so many divergent thoughts swirl through my thinking that ultimately I am compelled to ask *You* to help me in expressing my gratitude to *You*! — although You, the Giver, could assume that the recipient should have no need of coming to You again for help in thanking You! Oh, my soul becomes inconsolable when sin gains such a hold on me that it leads me into a new sin. I do not know how to address You. With each attempt I seem to alienate myself further. What impudence it is for me to come to You for consolation and guidance when it is against *You* that I have sinned! And yet, I know this does not displease You, for in a way this is a sign of my spiritual growth and progress. If sin has complete control over a man, he cannot think of You at all. It is when one has light regard for the gravity of his offense that he seeks to battle it with his own powers and so, is defeated. It is when he considers that You are on his side and that it is Your concern that he overcome, that he can triumph over all that happens to him.

* * * * *

Kierkegaard's Theology Of Prayer

*Prayer: Man's Victorious Surrender
To God!*

Chapter 7

The Loser Has Only
One Hope Of Victory!

Who would want to go to battle if there were no hope of conquering, and who would not go joyously if he were sure in advance of victory? My dear hearer, call him who is filled with the love of battle to the struggle and show him that the day of battle is so favorable and the conditions so auspicious that the hope of victory can be changed into certitude. Assure him, that though he is, to be sure, very brave; nevertheless, the victory remains uncertain as long as it has not been won. Tell him that the adversary is so feeble that the battle will be a simple joy. However, the most certain victory is in doubt as long as the contest has not yet been decided.

But if the outcome is never certain before the battle is joined, the combatant enters the struggle with a measure of apprehension. Yet, there is a condition to the struggle which removes apprehension and which gives the warrior true joy and courage; and this condition is that kind of victory where the combatant surrenders!

Not to waste our time in idle conjecture, is it possible that defeat can be equated with victory and thus assure that victory is certain? If men were to be summoned together and told: "I invite you to the battle, or rather, to the victory" and if one added, "Victory is so certain that defeat is victory or to be conquered is to be conqueror," what kind of incentive would that be for a man to engage in the struggle?

But if one went further and said, "Everyone can come and participate; no one is excluded, and all are victors," with what eagerness the crowd would gather and with what joyous enthusiasm! But if these men who desired to do battle demanded of the haranguer that he state the precise place where one might find such a field of battle, the place thus capable of inflaming one's courage, and he were to respond: "The field of battle is the inner sanctum of each one's soul; therefore, it would be better if each one were to return to his own place and to his own affairs in order to undertake the struggle," only one of the vast crowd would follow his advice. The multitude would not disperse but, seeing him now in a different light, would remain like an assembly of ninnies to ridicule his foolish chatter.

And if he were asked again the nature of this "battle," and he responded, "in prayer," there would no longer be any need to discuss the matter further, for prayer is the exact opposite of war. It is the affair of lazy ones and poltroons, best left to women and children, since battle is the pleasure of men.

And if, to the question of how to know what the nature of victory is, he responded: "In recognizing that one has lost," even the most morose could not refrain from laughter. How ludicrous it is to seek to justify the use of the word "loss" as being other than waste, failure, defeat, and to seek to do so by giving it the noble and elevated label of "triumph" in a figurative sense.

When the crowd has tired of its sport and its laughter, then the spokesman can draw a moral from the entire affair in words filled with spirit and conviction: that he is of the contrary opinion and that, for him at least, he prefers to be conqueror in the ordinary sense and the loser in the figurative sense.

My dear listener, is that all not a true picture of what life is all about? When the word "victory" is shouted into the air, it brings men together, fills them with a cheap enthusiasm, but the profound explanation of its true nature frightens them; and when a cost is mentioned, as it should be when it is a question of the supreme good, mockery ensues, simply because defeat and rout are given the appearance of a magnificent victory. Mockery does not always bring out the best in life, for it is scornful to pretend that things sacred and sublime can be purchased at bargain prices as can worldly goods, even though there is an abundance of merchandise on hand. On the other hand, it may be a pleasant thought that one can purchase that which is supremely good at low cost, but one is making a mistake since the price of such never varies. When one buys the best, it is pure obstinacy for any to conclude that *any* price is too high. One cannot pay too high a price, for no one has ever yet fathomed what the true price is for the supreme good. If one does pay too much, it is because he could not otherwise procure it. That is why it is pleasing and edifying to find recorded in the Gospel (Matthew 13:45, 46), and also recorded in actual experience, an account of a man who does not stand haggling over some purchase, computing conjunctures, ultimately paying too dearly for what the simplest of simpletons, at a chance, buys cheaply the next day. Once a person understands what the supreme good is, he is willing to give up everything in order to possess it. It brings comfort and assurance to see such a person live in peace and serenity because he has made such a conclusive decision. By gaining what he so ardently sought, he has added to his worldly acquisitions all that which he believes to be the true good of life. He treasures and keeps what he has gained and can be persuaded by no foil or flattery, by no craft or cunning, that he has paid too high a price. He stands alone in his resolve to pay the supreme price for the best. This noble resolve is less the fruit of prolonged deliberation than it is a most profound propulsion that is motivated by love for the highest and best. Carnal man does not understand this impulse. He does not understand what constitutes the "good fight," the noble quest, the lordly and spiritual victory. Nor does he want to! But God be praised, the child of simplicity, the infant in wisdom, comprehends! Few, indeed, are those who in the mature wisdom of middle age comprehend what the one who is only a babe in wisdom and knowledge has learned. In his egoism carnal man has too small a heart to encompass the grandeur and the glory of the greatest that life has to offer. In vain would anyone seek to converse with such a man and try to persuade him of the highest value. He would conclude that he is being led on by fraudulent pretensions of kindness. Consequently the supreme good becomes defaced, and, to his way of thinking, becomes the exact opposite of what it really is.

Chapter 8

Virtue Is The Highest Degree Of Wisdom, And Wisdom Is Merciful.

It is and always will be true that virtue is the highest degree of wisdom. It is equally certain that carnal man is minded to seek wisdom and to apply it. But if, to the man who seeks it, someone were to reveal that the highest degree of wisdom is virtue, then he would have to change his whole concept of true wisdom or it would never lead to virtue.

It is also true that clemency is the dullest of vengeances and, as one wise man of long ago observed, that the worst punishment for offenses is to overlook them. What confusion, what apprehension if a person, thirsting for revenge, should disguise his viciousness in the cloak of reconciliation! Would he thereby come anywhere near the beautiful virtue of clemency! Nothing is more certain than that the good man finds his recompense in clemency. But if, for this reason, the carnal man who is thirsty for revenge should pretend to do good, is he exercising his wisdom? The surest obligation in life is to fulfill one's duty — there is no question about that. But what about duty that demands sacrifice? No, in such a case one should renounce all dependence on calculation, fortuity, and even wisdom. He should want to do good because it is good; no other reason is needed. He has his recompense in the knowledge that he ought to fulfill his duty because it is duty. He can be certain, then, that his conduct is right; his reconciliation with his adversary is a consequence of the blind compulsion of the heart. Such a victory in reconciliation compels the victor to surrender his victory!

One can say much the same thing about wisdom, the object of his discourse being to understand how he who fights with integrity in prayer wins the battle in losing it. If a man does not wish to accept this resolute conclusion, if he has the audacity of heart to frustrate God by refusing to divest himself of his worldly manner of thinking; if, instead of taking this one decisive step, he casts aside the wisdom that God proffers, in no way would any discourse dissuade him. There is such a thing as "inverse cosmometry" where one seeks to reap before he sows, where he wishes to make a judgment before he understands, a susceptibility to believe that blessing always follows action. But what does it avail if, with mouth full of wise sayings and empty heart, he circumvents God and refuses to accept the dictum that it is necessary to lose everything in order to gain everything, and in coldness of soul simply refuses to even try God's way? Also, all his agonizing in prayer, all the vain struggles which have him on the very edge of annihilation, and all his leaning on divine grace bring only temporary gain. No art of rhetoric will bring him to even a momentary desistance in the conviction that burns in him. Even should an angel speak to him in heavenly tongue and extol the effectual prayers of the righteous, it would not sway the carnal man. For what good is it for one to hear the word, even spoken by an angel of God, if there is disbelief!

Our discourse has not less importance if we indicate that our entire motive is profit. In doing so, we do take a risk. Anyone who has an interest in this life has reason for interest in the life to come. But when any man seeks to describe his treasure in that life to come, it may not help since he is seeking to reveal that which his heart comprehends but which is an enigma to the man who has given no thought to such things. No man who is convinced and convicted of the Eternal can influence one of contrary opinion, for one cannot force his conviction about that which is eternal upon another. In the sanguine comfort of his success and his prosperity he never for one moment supposes that his faith is an illusion. Although carnal man, in hostility to the very suggestion of the existence of the divine, dispels God from his thinking as being mere illusion and sorcery and phantasmagoria, God comes back to him with the message of salvation through annihilation. Our discourse, then, endeavors to seize the opportunity to promulgate this edifying thought: True prayer is a struggle with God where one triumphs *through the triumph of God!*

Chapter 9

You May Struggle With Failure, But Not With Him Who Overcomes Failure!

To struggle in prayer, what a contradiction! What is there that is prestigious enough to bring together these two words, "prayer," "struggle," which demand to be coupled together? In all combat the first prerequisite is to determine the nature of the fighting forces. If prayer is the matter under discussion, combat is impossible because prayer is not a weapon of war; on the contrary, it is a tranquil transaction of peace. It is not the modus operandi of the assailant or of the defender, but of him who surrenders himself. And if, as a good tactician, he considers the remoteness of the adversaries, combat is still impossible, for when one does not pray, God remains in the heavens and man on earth, and the distance between is then too great; but when one prays, God and man draw very near each other, and there is no interspace which one can define as the field of battle. For if a man surrenders himself completely in prayer, he does not fight; but if he does not surrender himself at all, he is not praying even though he remain day and night on his knees!

It is the same circumstance as when a man corresponds with a friend who is at a distance: if he does not take care to write the address correctly, the letter will not reach its destination, and relationships will not be established in spite of the repeated mailings. Likewise, he who prays ought to take care that the form of his address is correct, that it be the wholehearted surrender of himself; otherwise, he does not pray to God.

Moreover, he ought to give heed to the fact that He Who examines our hearts is under no illusion. For kings and princes may escape to the solitude of the country in order to get away from the throngs that are constantly harassing them with urgent and unreasonable requests. But our God, whose dwelling is in the heavens, is better protected, although He is the Being who is actually nearest to each one of us. All prayer that is not clothed in true and authentic dress, that genuine raiment of the serious heart, does not reach Him at all. Then, although He is near enough to hear the feeblest sigh, it does not concern Him because it is not addressed to the Proper Person.

It is impossible for prayer to be used as a weapon against God, for only the genuine prayer reaches Him. He does not even hear the false. Therefore, it is far from possible for one to use prayer against another. A man can, conceivably, use prayer against another. Between adversaries prayer could be a terrible weapon, perhaps the most deadly. Without reservations, the brave is exhorted not to abuse his power against the feeble, but the feeble is also urged not to abuse the power he might have in prayer against the brave. The tyrant who abuses his power or the deceiver who misuses his cleverness can never commit as flagrant an injustice as can the man whose shameful, perfidious and misplaced imprecations are in revilement directed against the heart of another. Such behavior would be improper in God's sight. The man who takes joy in such proceedings is treading the very edge of the brink of contumely and disgrace.

Under what circumstance can it be said that one is *battling* in prayer? Is a man at war when he takes issue with One with Whom his relationship is intimate and profound, especially if he wishes to protect that relationship? Our natural impulse is to praise the pious and simple prayer of the little child, for he is humble in spirit and sees God as One with Whom he is never in conflict. It is in this that the virtue of the child consists. But also it is this that reflects immaturity in one's surrender to God. The child, reared in the Saviour's teaching, asks God for that which is good and thanks Him when good is received; but what has he asked for and what has he received?

When he receives a toy at Christmas, he thanks God from Whom he has requested that gift. It would be strange, indeed, if he were not convinced that God is generous, since at the Christmas season there is a grateful spirit in the home anyway. It is the same at any time and on every occasion when the child prays and in consequence receives a blessing.

On the other hand, the child does not associate the sad, the tragic, the disagreeable with God, for the child spirit sees only the good and the desirable. Why, then, be astounded that God is all generosity in the eyes of the infant? The child reasons that anything which is unpleasant can be attributed to the intervention of the wicked, something that can only be accounted for as being the activity of an evil person. If the child perceives sadness and torment in the comportment of his mother, he never dreams that God has any responsibility in her sorrow. Nor does he have any incertitude about God's nearness and support. Immediately the child attributes the vexation to wicked people. If death takes his father and he witnesses the sorrow of the mother, he has no concept of the nature of death even though the gravity and import of it may cast a shadow over his whole existence. But if he is given a new suit, his mother cannot help but smile through tears at his joy over the gift, and this only complicates his reaction to death. When the mourning mother explains in tenderness that his father is with God in heaven, the child is quickly reconciled with God and here, as in other matters, he sees even death as God's blessing. This explanation, which initially is nothing more than the guileful artifice of maternal love as is the custom in explaining to small children, little by little, in some strange way, also brings comfort to the mother and consoles her in her grief.

Thus the child surmounts the obstacle of death when it stands in his way. The father was with him in his earthly life, and it was the good fortune of the child to know and experience paternal love as he expected it to be. Now the father is in heaven, very near to God. The child can only conjecture about the true nature of the change that has come to be. One thing he does not do: he does not impute that death to God. When you consider the childish fear of God, you need to use sound judgment always. This inner assurance that the child treasures is a praiseworthy attribute that anyone ought to cherish and retain until the day of his death. For him God is truly alive and present in every thought that he thinks and in every breath that he takes. But at the same time, in another way of looking at it, the concept that the child has formed of God is not exactly theological.

The difficulty begins when it is necessary to reconcile conflicting circumstances, as when the mourning spouse feels a need to confront God in her bereavement and seek from Him an explanation that is, for her, more adequate and acceptable than the one that came so readily to her lips when she was comforting her child. This difficulty arises only when one is more mature and needs to bring, not just the good and the joyous and the beautiful, but also the opposite to God (if there is a God and a divine profundity to life!).

At this point if this childish way of looking at things resurfaces, we are no longer satisfied with puerile and simplistic explanations but desire more mature elucidation. Would one praise an adult who fears God so much that he makes no distinction between the desirable and the undesirable, the pleasant and the unpleasant, returning thanks for whatever is given? No poor wretch would need to struggle in prayer if everything happened according to his liking. Should this be the case, then if his desires were not granted, he would renounce prayer, thus acting contrary to his inner conviction that all ought to be brought to God if you wish to comprehend His ways. However, it may be that our true inner nature being carnal, we are no match for outer circumstances, and these outer circumstances make it more difficult to admit that God is not human and carnal, but spiritual and supernal. If man renounces this inner light, then he can no longer engage in the great conquest that is prayer! His battle takes on a far different aspect, bravely pushing defiance to its limit and denying God, thinking thereby to destroy Him altogether. In his childishness he assumes that he can humiliate God, suggesting that God will come to regret His actions, but then it will be too late.

Further, although he has never found those who refuse to admit that there is a God, he has encountered those who, in their self-importance, think that God cannot do without them. They are like the spoiled child who wishes he could do without his father, but who in his self-conceit believes that his father cannot do without him!

The foes we meet in life are many and their diversity necessitates God's help in the struggle. If we struggle against God, then our prayers are useless as a means to confront our foes. We may use different methods of approach to God in order to gain His help. The spirit and attitude with which we approach Him must be one that is firmly grounded in our belief that He will help and that He will give success. If one were to suggest to us that God is fickle and that He is far from us and our needs, we would rebel, for that is to make of this ever-present, ever-loving One a distant and an unapproachable monster. The worst and most abominable blasphemy is to speak of God as though He were inhuman, unfeeling, uncaring. No, God to Whom we pray has a heart to feel our yearnings, ears to hear our complaints, even as does our closest fellow being, only more so! If He does not immediately grant all our desires, He does not dwell less near nor is He left untouched by our cries or by our pleadings or by our misery when we are abandoned and alone. He is instant in His anticipation of our requests and prompt in His joy of granting answers. He is moved by the lamentations of the one who struggles; and when that striving soul succumbs in disheartenment and founders in the whirlpool of vicissitudes, and when it seems that all is lost, then that grace and love which all the ages have sung about in their praises are bestowed in limitless measure by Him Who reigns in limitless love!

Chapter 10

The Consummate Strategy Of The Pray-er Lies In His Victorious Surrender To God!

But, you will ask, what is the final outcome of this struggle that is prayer? This demand is not a casual and random reaction. Actually, there is both eager anticipation and fear at what the response will be. Even a partial explanation can provide consolation. Perhaps we do not need every detail laid bare, for we have already been told the result: *He who struggles in prayer gains the victory when God is triumphant and that is to pray truly and effectively; that is what makes one a true man of prayer.*

My dear hearer, have you never conversed with a man who, surpassing you greatly in wisdom, appears kindly disposed toward you and is even more anxious about your welfare than you yourself are? If not, I am going to reveal it to you now. Remember how in the beginning of our deliberations we were in complete disagreement with the sage because it seemed to me that his views were peculiarly his alone. However, I had confidence in him. I believed that in spite of his superior knowledge, he would be open-minded and would strive to remove the disagreement between us. Oh, to be sure, we did exchange idle remarks in our verbal joustings. Nevertheless, the sage was able to maintain uncommitted neutrality even though he could not help but notice that I was carried away because I thought it was highly important that he accept my point of view. I was not so much concerned with the exactitude of my opinion as I was with impressing the sage that I was in complete control of the discussion.

Finally, after many prolonged twistings and turnings in our speculations, when it seemed to me that I was defining my position with great clarity and believed that he would therefore accept my explanation, he shook his finger at me and said: "The opinion that you have expressed is exactly what I said in the beginning, when you neither were able nor seemed to want to understand me." Then shame swept over me and I was embarrassed by my earlier attitude, although it did not take away from the joy I felt in finally arriving at the truth of the matter. I realized that I had not conquered the sage, but had myself been conquered.

What an astonishing adventure! I had actually rejoiced in my restraint at not being carried away so as to direct my insults toward the wise man who was showing me more love than I understood. Embarrassment saved me from interrupting my true battle, which is in prayer, and directing my hostility toward the sage as if he were the enemy when, in spite of my offensive challenge to his wisdom and understanding, he was aiding me to find the truth on my own.

That is what happens to the combatant when he does not renounce his closely-guarded preconceived notions, which renunciation is an absolute requisite for continuing the struggle we call prayer. It is only pious imagination to pretend otherwise. Men become lukewarm or even cold and indifferent when they overlook the true nature of prayer. It is not merely for the sake of demanding God's help in our needs. Only dissemblers, imposters, and insolent people think so. The chief end of life is not being able to manage our own affairs in this world, using prayer as a means to that end. If that were so, our demands on God would be no more than idle chatter. On the contrary, the man of prayer says: "O Lord, my God, I have nothing in particular to ask of You. Even if You were to promise to grant each of my desires, I would not know how to formulate those desires, except to ask the blessed privilege of keeping near You, as near as possible in this present world where we live insulated, isolated lives, and absolutely near You throughout eternity."

And if one's gaze is heavenward as he prays that prayer, expressing such a desire, is not he the true man of prayer, he who seeks God only? It is here that it is necessary to renounce any preconceived notion. For these errant desires, these carnal lusts, the cares of this world are but temporal and temporary things and generally die away before man himself dies. If he does not reach out, then, to seize what is eternal, how can he persevere in prayer? When desire becomes less and less burning and wears itself out, and when the serpent of lust is destroyed also, then there is no need for continued vigilance, and inner restraints against the things that tempt us are no longer needed.

And now, who is the victor? God, from whom we have not succeeded in wresting the answers we demand to our prayers. But in the very act of praying we also have been victors, for to triumph is to corroborate the truth that even when we are wrong, God still is love. To acknowledge Him and be thankful to Him only when He grants some earthly desire, which we regard as the supreme good, is to make an idol of Him.

What kind of victory is it in which the state of those who have conquered does not differ from that of those who have fought and lost? Has God changed? It seems difficult to give an affirmative answer to such a query, and yet for all that, it is so. God has changed, although it has always appeared that He is unchangeable. However, this immutability does not take the form of a glacial indifference, a sublimity which kills, an ambiguous remoteness which callous reason vaunts. No, on the contrary, this immutability is profound, warm, omnipresent. It consists in being concerned with man; and that is why it is not altered by the cry of the suppliant, as if the end were at hand and, defenseless, all one can do is resort to a cowardly withdrawal.

And he who prays, has he changed? Yes, that is not difficult to see. For he has become a true man of prayer who always triumphs, which is one and the same thing. He already had the assurance of victory in his prayers, although it was a tenuous assurance in that he had the inner conviction that his prayer would be heard if he prayed for the right things. Now he has changed. It is still true that, imperfect as his praying has been, it has still been profitable for him because it has aided him in concentrating his soul on his desire. Unfortunately, he has entertained too many vague cravings so that his heart is tossed by every wind of desire. But now in praying he has become selective and does not squander God's assurance of help on every worthless longing that crosses his path. Rather, he renounces all lesser longings and musters all his resources to obtain that one pearl of great price, that one treasure that God wants to give him. Thus, he is prepared to throw himself into the struggle with God and triumph, for he has become the man who truly prays, that is, truly hurls himself into the "struggle with God," which prayer is, and is victor through the victory of God!

On the field of battle, when the front line wins the victory, those in the second ranks do not need to fight. All they do is share in the celebration of the victory. This is not so in the realm of the spirit. Even though all the forces are not needed to win the victory, yet it is urgent that all our forces should be mustered in order that all may know what it means to triumph through losing. How numerous are the contending powers! And how often the real struggle is within! If it were an open battle, nothing would be left to speculation. The one who prays is not seeking anything that is perceivable. He is not at all concerned with appearances. He does not need to explain his desires to God, for he has renounced desire. What he is really struggling for in prayer is to be wonderfully changed. He does not believe that this transformation is to be gained without effort. Throughout the hustle and bustle of his working hours and also in the quiet of the night he works and is not idle. Even in those moments of debility he cannot free himself from this furious activity of prayer, but labors on and on, seeking that transformation. Even sorrow and grief are an advantage to him if they become the bridge over which he passes to that Divine Friendship which he covets. Even the gathering shadows of twilight are an advantage if he can meet God in the thick darkness that is before him. Even the incomprehensible and the unknown are a boon, for they require faith. For here is true and genuine faith: our anguishes, our trials, our failures, our defeats are not intended as the mockery of God. Faith makes it all clearer than actual knowledge ever could, although it appears to our outward gaze as being the worst thing that could ever happen to us. God does not sell out to us in order to escape embarrassment. "He is unchangeable?" mocks the one who has given up the struggle and has surrendered to lethargy and stodginess. But the immutability that is apparent to us is a refusal to fulfil the trivialities of the moment.

There is a tremendous faith revealed here. To our eyes it encompasses the most urgent and difficult steps. When does the Comforter come? For the saddened disciples whom He had guided in their apprenticeship under Him, Christ spoke the words: "Ye have heard how I said unto you, I go away ..." (John 14:28). What did it all mean? It meant that they were losing all that they had. He was their special companion. He was their daily bread of joy. He was their one hope for happiness. No rich man who has lost everything, no lover who is bereft of his beloved, no man who has seen all hope vanish out of his life has ever become as poor as the disciples became then. However, it was necessary that Christ leave them; "that is advantageous to you," He told them (John 16:7). From a mere human point of view the disciple does not understand. How can he understand?

Then comes the Comforter. When does He come? Is it immediately, as we might want to demand? Was it *immediately* for the disciples? Was it *immediately* for Abraham when he was compelled to wait for seventy years? O blessed be that man who knows how to comfort the afflicted, who knows how to sustain the one whose legs are trembling and whose knees are buckling, who knows how to guide the one who is blinded by his misery and is without hope in the world. Cursed be all the vague discourses which pretend to bridge the chasm of our afflictions, which give the appearance of consolation but lack the power of it. Cursed be all those seducing words which charm the ears with their pretentious elegance, but leave a nauseating taste in the mouth of him who speaks them and a dissonant ring of bewildered dismay in the ears of the one who hears them. No, the Comforter does not come immediately; and the only thing a man can say to himself and to others is that *He is coming! He is coming,* as truly as God lives!

The Comforter comes, then, to bring a complete change in our life, a transformation. He renders all things new. He takes from the afflicted the garment of sorrow and gives to him a new heart and a renewed spirit. However, it all requires time. Even when the one who struggles in prayer comes to believe that all is lost, he is really deceiving himself, and were he to lapse into empty trust in the ways of man and in worldly powers, there would still be time. For the man who is defiant, who is misled by the many unfortunate turns of fate, may seek to make a mockery of the one who trusts in nothing more than the love of God. But how many are the sorrows and misfortunes that can still be helped and healed; and the one who had concluded that all is lost is marvellously saved! All this aids in this inner transformation.

One struggles in order to attain transformation, and prayer is the instrument whereby it is attained. Such a person rejects the idea that he himself of his own power has brought about the transformation. No, all that happens is providential; all comes from God and is sent to purify the one who loves Him. Another struggles in prayer in order that his fault might be laid bear, not out of any opportunistic desire that admission of his guilt will profoundly sweeten the reconciliation. Rather, he desires that the whole transaction might put him in harmony with the human race and thus have universal value. Another designs that it set him apart from society and doom him to sorrow and solitude, an exceptional choice, to be sure. The combatant struggles thus with God in prayer, or with himself, invoking in his supplication the help of God against himself.

But if the combatant does not renounce this inner compulsion and does not cease to pray, if he loves God profoundly and longs ardently for That One without Whom a person is nothing, if he longs as ardently for Him as for One through Whom a person becomes all, if he acknowledges his indebtedness to God for the ever-growing wisdom and reverence that come his way, that one will be able to give thanks for it all, even while he struggles in prayer. Although the answers will come only at an hour that God alone knows, and if it is necessary in the meantime to purchase additional oil for the lamp of hope, it is none the less certain that we have not been deceived in our transactions with God, for we discover after a time that we have obtained the Pearl of Great Price. Although it appears exorbitant, one has not paid too dearly, nor will he ever regret the cost, for it is not a trifling that he has gained, but that which has the guarantee of God behind it!

If a man takes seriously what the wise person knows is true today, tomorrow and forever, that when you lose this guarantee, you lose everything, and if he renounces the world and all worldly ways, he ought not regard as regrettable the bargain he has made because it strengthens his relationship with God. To do the important thing and to impress on others what is important is not to part company with God; it is simply to free oneself from the worthless pursuit of the frivolous and the profane.

If it is true that a man has really renounced all, he will not have to regret the bargain he has made, but it is true only if he has really *renounced* it and not lost it. To renounce and to lose are two different things. As a consequence of the confidence and fellowship of God that he has gained, one can be forever grateful to God that he has been delivered from the childish snatching after trivial things and the infantine frivolity that obstructs his comprehension of what is truly significant.

But let us see now the result. My dear listener, picture the child who with the crayon scribbles out at random disorderly lines, the invention of his fantasy. Behind him, but invisible, stands the gifted artist who guides his hand so that the design, seemingly destined to trail off into chaos, of a sudden unfolds in a pattern of beauty, and the meandering line takes on the wonder of harmony and loveliness. Imagine the astonishment of the child.

Or think what happens when in the evening, the child lays aside the scribbled patchwork, only to discover that while he is asleep a friendly hand corrects and perfects his formless sketch. Imagine his surprise when he glimpses his work in the morning! It is the same with man: for let us not forget that even the adult retains some traits of childhood. And in prayer he perceives a means of gaining this transformation. The young man cherishes the thought of what he may become in this world and he chooses an example from among the great and noble spirits of the past. As he matures, he puts aside childish thoughts and is no more concerned with the superficial. He wants to see his life take substantial form after the image of God and not in imitation of some mortal's nature. He then seeks to determine how great is the line of demarcation, delineating how closely he comes to resembling God. But alas! The difference is so great that, whereas the child needs only an added something to what is already there, he on the other hand is, in the sight of God, nothing! He is aware that if he is to approach the image of God (and that is the only goal he desires), then he must be willing to be reduced to nothing in order that God may inundate his whole being with divine light in such a way that he resembles God.

When the sea unchains its fury and tosses and heaves, it cannot reflect the sky nor can it mirror accurately the least movement. But when calm is restored and the sea becomes serene and bottomless, the image of the sky is graven clearly in its depths.

And now, who is the victor? God, for He has not acceded to the supplicant's demands; He has not given what the pray-er sought. But the pray-er has also triumphed. It is not the victory of having God bestow upon him an *explanation* of God's ways; rather, it is a *transformation* into God's image.

Finally, what is the nature of this victory in which the nature of the conqueror differs from that of the combatant? Has God become different? It seems difficult to respond affirmatively and it is so, especially if the supplicant assumes the wrong idea of God and no longer seeks transformation. Has the prayer changed? Yes, for he has a different understanding of the nature of prayer and, moreover, he is so grateful that he cannot restrain himself from praying without ceasing. And he who prays without ceasing is the true man of prayer and to pray without ceasing means to be the eternally triumphant one!

And this continuous persistent and persisting thanksgiving, should it ever cease? No, assuredly; there is always a reason to thank God. Each person is in debt to Him, eternally so! But alas! the debt which a man contracts at the table of chance, at the throw of the dice, at the dealing of cards, is called "a debt of honor." I console myself with the thought that this is an absurdity. Why hasten to give such a debt an honorable designation and leave it at that? The debt we owe to God is not a debt of honor of this striation; rather, it is an honor to be in debt to God, an honor to owe nothing to chance, an honor to owe nothing to fate, an honor to owe nothing to caprice, but to owe all things all the time and everywhere to God, our Father! It is thus that he prays truly who struggles in prayer and triumphs through the triumph of God.

We have spoken of combat. In general, it does not have a joyous ending; the triumph of the one is the crushing of the other, and sometimes it even happens that both are losers. But the battle of which we are speaking, the battle we call prayer, is marvelous and worthy of being tried, worthy of being loved, worthy of being eternally celebrated; for prayer is a battle in which both fight and both win. Moreover, a battle between loved ones usually ends in love re-doubled!

If, my dear reader, you object that this discourse is difficult to comprehend (and perhaps the afflicted one finds it to be a very inadequate explanation and without validity, when related to his suffering), the battle is not an easy one. If there are some who are bewildered, having expected a more plausible explanation of prayer as conflict, the fault is not in this discourse. One must expect victory only in the sublime and noble connotation of the word rather than in a figurative interpretation, since sorrow and suffering are not figurative things.

But when the hour of victory will come, no one knows. But one thing we do know: this battle of prayer is a struggle for life or death! The victory is for eternity!

Prayers In The Existential Mode

The existential meanderings of Kierkegaard are like artesian spouts of spiritual fountains that well up in our hearts and spring to our lips in prayer. Following are prayers inspired by gleanings from some of his most notable statements. Nothing is more indicative of the power of a person's prayer-life than the degree to which that person inspires prayer in you!

Chapter 11

Prayers
From The Depths
"Out of the depths
have I cried unto Thee."

(In his *Purity Of Heart Is To Will One Thing* Kierkegaard states, "At dances and at other festive occasions our worldly judgment contends that the
more the musicians and the louder the music, the
better. But when we are considering that which is
divine, the deeper the stillness, the better.")

O God of this world and the next, our sports, our games, our
worldly pursuits and competitions demand the shouts and
cheers of the crowds and the plaudits of the multitudes. But
when we forsake our strivings for recognition and fame and
seek only Your approbation and Your pleasing, then we need
the still dews of Your quietness and the silent but cleansing
breezes of Your Holy Spirit moving among us and within us.
Long have we been cajoled by the bland blandishments of those
who have tried to dissuade us from following Your way and
have sought to persuade us that there are joy and peace and
pleasures that only the world can give. Now we need to listen
to the Still Small Voice that speaks from the great depth of
eternal treasures and calls us to the pursuit of a peace and a
power that the world with all its tumult cannot give. In our
weakness we wait on You, O Lord, to renew our strength!
Amen.

* * * * *

("What I lack," SK writes in his *Journal,* "is to be clear in my mind *what I am to do,* not what I am to know." What good does it do to discover truth, or understand all systems of philosophy, or be able to explain the mysteries of life, if all this knowledge is not to be caught up in the fabric of every facet of my being and woven into living character? My soul longs for that "as the African desert thirsts for water.")

You have told us, O Master, that whoever does Your will shall know of Your teaching, whether it be of God or whether You speak only the cliches and commonplaces of another man. Our feet stumble until they walk in Your way; our arms hang listlessly at our sides until we reach them out in warm, embracing love; our hands are numb and unfeeling until they are stretched forth in healing ministry and helpful ministrations. Let us not love in words only, we pray, but in deeds and so, in truth! The least, the lowest, the last, the lost wait for a Comforter, a Healer, a Companion, and a Guide. Move us to hasten to their aid, for inasmuch as we do it unto the least of these, we do it unto Thee. Amen.

* * * * *

(SK points out that we confess, not so that God will know us better, but "so that we will know ourselves better." There is no point in confessing to the Omniscient, the all-knowing God, what He already knows better than we ourselves do. But man does not realize what dark thoughts and evil inclinations lie beneath the surface of our artificial, superficial sophistication. A person can act in passion, even in ignorance, and commit atrocious misdeeds and yet "know not what he does!")

"Out of the depths have I cried unto Thee, O God" — and it is truly "out of the depths." I know not what hidden fires may burn within this oft-times rebellious heart of mine, what cruel and bitter consequences may come of those fires, what destruction, what heartache, what irreparable tragedy. But this I do know: when I come before You and confront Your tender mercies, it is impossible to overlook the purity, the holiness, the perfect love in Whose Presence I kneel. All the righteousness that I might take pride in of a sudden appears only as filthy rags. The resentment and the hate that I harbor, the envy of those who prosper, the self-justification with which I excuse the evil that I do and the extenuating manner in which I absolve myself of guilt for the good I fail to do — all, all are invisible to me until I witness Your great mercy and love. Then I recall the Price You paid on the Cross to reveal that love to sinners. Lord, I believe; help Thou my unbelief. Lord, I repent; forgive my utter ignorance of my need. All this I ask for the sake of the One Who paid the Price. Amen.

* * * * *

(As early as 1838 SK wrote in his *Journal* that if Christ were to come and take up residence in his heart, He will have to come as He came to the disciples in the upper room after the resurrection, for "Christ entered, the doors being locked!" Much as we need and much as we say we want Him, we too often keep our hearts closed to His coming; and we are hostile if He stays too long!)

O God, take Jesus back! We did not want Him to stay with us as a living presence. Long ago Zacharias said, "Blessed be the Lord God of Israel, for He hath visited and redeemed His people." A *visit* we can accommodate, but an abiding Presence? That miraculous birth in that stable in Bethlehem when beautiful stars shone down and the angels sang their carols lent a lovely touch to the year, but we were not ready for all those rigid demands that He made, once He was no longer the tiny Child of Christmas. How we rejoiced when He pronounced all those "blessings" on the poor, those that mourn, those who hunger and thirst, those who seek peace, because we are poor and sad and hungry and thirsty and tired of the turmoil and strife of the world. But why did He follow all that with, "Whosoever would be my disciple, let him take up his cross and follow me"? He even told us to "be perfect as your Father in heaven is perfect." And we can't do it, God; we can't measure up — so take Him back! Or, if He is to stay, grant us *power to become*, which He said He would give "to as many as receive him!" Amen.

*   *   *   *   *

(SK admitted that time and again he was overwhelmed by the tremendous powers and the seemingly-unlimited expanses of nature, the mountains whose vastnesses were immeasurable, the oceans whose wide-ranging waters were incomprehensible, and the heavens stretching beyond the reaches of man's imagination. Yet he marvelled again and again at the sureness of the flight of the birds, whether they were moving about in the mountains' ranges or soaring over the ocean-waves or mounting to the very heavens. All at once he realized how very small he was and how very great, how small in his own eyes and in comparison with this massive world, but how great in the eyes of the Heavenly Father, and in heavenly computations!)

How much more precious we are to you, O Father, than many sparrows. Your Son has told us so. If not one sparrow falls to the ground without Your notice, then we are sure that not one of us, Your children, will go astray without Your precious and parental concern. Let us express our faith and trust in You by using the thoughts of another who, seeing the confidence and assurance with which the water fowl struck out into the fog-dimmed skies, exclaimed,

He who from zone to zone
Guides through the boundless sky thy certain flight,
In the long way that I must tread alone
Will lead my steps aright!

You will, O Father! That is not only our faith, but it is Thy promise. That promise is that You, the Eternal God, are our refuge and underneath are the Everlasting Arms. No child of Thine ever yet has fallen lower than Thy "underneath!" Praise be to Your Holy Name! Amen.

*   *   *   *   *

(In July 1837, SK must have been thinking back over his life as an unhappy and frustrated schoolboy when he wrote, "Many people reach their conclusions about life and its problems like some of us schoolboys: they cheat their teacher by copying the answer out of a book instead of working it out for themselves, as the instructor has commanded.")

Our Master Teacher, we often try to solve life's problems and meet life's needs with words instead of works. Along with New Testament writer James we discover that even faith without works is dead. Certainly, words without works are dead, too. Even as the Eternal Word became flesh in our Lord Jesus Christ and moved with healing wonder among us, so our words of comfort, encouragement, and forgiveness must come to life in what we do, or all these remain dead, buried in the stony mausoleum of compassion unexpressed save in lifeless symbols. No longer O God, is our Lord Jesus Christ shut up in a book or prisoned in a creed; but He has come to live in the hearts of men, to move in the lives of men, to embrace with their arms and minister with their hands. Accept these hands of mine, O Lord; accept these arms of mine, accept this life of mine! I offer all in Thy service. Amen.

*   *   *   *   *

(Because he believed that "one must know one's self before he can know anyone or anything else," SK spent years in the fruitless search for self and came up empty. Of a sudden he discovered God, the immediate consequence of which was that he found his self, his *real* self, stripped of all pretense, stripped of all pharisaism. It was a sad discovery, a crushing revelation — one that he never could have endured had it not been that at the same instant he discovered God!)

How willing and eager we are, O God, to study those phenomena that lie at the greatest distance from us — the sun, the moon, the far reaches of outer space. We explore the mystery of tangled jungles and plunge beneath the unplumbed depths of sea and ocean. Yet we stand, hesitant and trembling, at the threshold of self as though we fear to pierce the tangled jungle of human thought or plunge into that dark, dark sea of emotional depths. For a lamp unto our feet and a light unto our path we turn to Thy Word and lo! — we behold as in a mirror what manner of man we are. Let us never turn away and forget what You have revealed to us, not only of ourselves but also of Your Self. We could not bear what we see there of self unless we catch a clear, authentic, and unfading glimpse of what You are and what You can do — what You can do with us and with the raw and worthless material we hold out to You when we offer our selves! Take us, break us, and then re-make us, Lord, after Your Likeness! Amen.

* * * * *

(In his *Journal* in 1854 SK pointed out that "Everything God makes is created out of nothing — and everything that God intends to use He first reduces to nothing." He is keenly aware of his own worthlessness. He describes himself as "slight, delicate, weak, denied in almost every respect the physical requirements in order to be able to pass for a complete man as compared with others . . ." But never did he doubt that God had use for him and a purpose for him.)

O great all-knowing, almighty, all-caring God, consider that I do not smirk or smile or consort with the learned scientist when he ridicules the thought that something can be made out of nothing. You did, indeed, in the very beginning take on a universe that was "without form and void," and in the darkness You said, "Let there be light," and there was light! Then every nook and cranny of this vast and formless nothing responded to the touch of Your miracle-working Hand. I had better believe that You can create something out of nothing, otherwise there is no hope for me! But miracle of miracles! Even before my life manifests anything of difference or change, I can feel the mighty thrust of Your Holy Spirit working within. You have given me "power to become," and that power is already at work, promising that I one day will be a full-grown child of Thine after the likeness and the fulness of Christ! Amen.

*   *   *   *   *

(SK often deplored the fact that the "in-and-for-itself" has gone out of life. This "in-and-for-itself" to him was the *absolute*, that which the New Testament demands and which no man can abrogate. It is the Law of God. "Thus saith the Lord!" In the realm of ethics, morals, and religion we have so lowered the barriers that even the swine can crawl over! This state of affairs, he says, has led man to claim that "the race has outgrown Christianity." Quite to the contrary, the race has gone backwards, and Christ is still far out ahead of us all and is beckoning to us to leave the pack, desert the multitude, and come and walk with Him, even though He is our only Companion!)

Yes, Jesus, You call to us over the tumult of life's wild and restless sea, and there is no peace or comfort for us unless we who are weary and heavy-laden hear and heed the call to come unto You! Purity is not lost to the world, even though it does have to wade through the mire and muck of human waste. Patience has not vanished from the earth, and we can still "wait on the Lord" and renew our strength, even in the midst of all the earthly tumult around us. The world has not been left desolate of deep and abiding joy, even though many attempt to discover it in empty and fruitless pursuit of pleasure. Help us now and always to walk in the Way that our Lord reveals, to believe the Truth that He proclaims, and to live and enjoy that fulness of the Life He gives. He is "in-and-for-itself," *absolutely*, the Way, the Truth, and the Life — and we follow! Amen.

* * * * *

(In his *Journal* SK speaks of "the *lover's understanding of God,* being able to do freely what at first I had to be compelled to do." We may do what another desires or even commands, but not out of love for that other. Indeed, the good or the favor may be done grudgingly, bitterly, often with resentment of the circumstances that oblige you to capitulate. But when anything must be done out of love for the beloved, nothing is too much to desire or ask!)

O Thou Who are Infinite Love, if it were only *Law* that demands our loyalty and our love, that loyalty and love might be so grudgingly given that the loyalty would be not loyalty, but apostasy, and that love might not be love but hate! If only the pressure of circumstances required that we be patient, how impatiently we would tarry and wait! But it is not the lowly law of human stricture or the abject enslavement of worldly circumstances that rules our hearts and so, orders our lives.

No, it is the very limited response of this poor and feeble love to the limitless Love of God; it is our desperate striving to open and receive His Unspeakable Gift which is really too great for our poor hearts! Heavenly Father, You so loved the world that our one and only return for Your blessings is the love of our poor hearts. Amen.

* * * * *

(Few people have ever been as conscious of, and contrite for, their sins, their complete unworthiness and worthlessness in the sight of God as was Kierkegaard. Yet, he was aware that Christ was beckoning to him as he groped for help and healing. In his *Training for Christianity* he expounds on our Lord's invitation: "Come hither, all ye poor and miserable ... ye who are despised and disdained ... ye sick, lame, deaf, blind, crippled, come hither! Ye bedridden, yea, come ye also hither: come! — Ye lepers." Then he goes deeper into human misery by including "Ye sick at heart, ye who only through pain learn to know that a man has a heart in a sense quite different from the heart of a beast." And the Lord's healing does not stop there: "The invitation stands at the parting of the ways where death separates life and life. Come hither, all ye sorrowful, all ye that travail in vain and are sore troubled!" SK, who himself suffered greatly in body and soul, was a trusting patient of the Great Physician.)

O Lord our God, we are victims, all of us, of those dire afflictions that have been the bane of all mankind all the time. Ills abound, some without our knowledge of the cause, many that we have brought upon ourselves. We give thanks that You have imparted to man the wisdom and the means to alleviate and even obliterate many of the scourges that imperil all existence. But even with these precious earthly skills we find that we cannot "minister to a mind diseased, pluck from the memory a rooted sorrow, raze out the written troubles of the brain," or "with some sweet oblivious antidote cleanse the stuff'd bosom of that perilous stuff which weighs upon the heart." O wretched people that we are! Who will deliver us? With everlasting praise and gratitude we turn to You, Great Physician, Who

> takes the suffering human race,
> Who reads each wound, each weakness clear —
> Who puts His finger on the place
> And says, "Thou ailest here and here."

Our hearts rejoice that You are more than diagnostician, You are Healer and Healing; You are the Remedy for every weakness and the Balm for every woe. Grant, then, that of Your wholeness we may all receive. Amen.

*   *   *   *   *

(One observation always troubled SK greatly: it was how those who serve the truth and the honorable always turn out badly in this life. "A true follower of Christ will soon be cast headlong out of this world. And if there comes another follower, the same will happen to him." But SK qualifies this gloomy summation of the career and fate of the man of truth and of honor by adding, "They have always come out badly in life, *as long as they lived,* and as soon as they are dead, they are deified!" He points out in *Purity of Heart* that "nothing in the world has been so completely lost as was Christianity at the time that Christ was crucified. And in the understanding of the moment, never in the world has anyone accomplished so little by the sacrifice of a consecrated life as did Jesus Christ. And yet in this same instant, eternally understood, he had accomplished all.")

From above and beyond us, O God, comes Your call to consider Your summons and to commit ourselves to You in love. Your call, from without, stirs our inner response to be Your prophet, not as foreteller, but as "forth-teller," courageously proclaiming Your truth to the world. No promise of joy, peace, contentment, and pride attends Your call. Indeed, even as You call, You suggest that we may be reviled, persecuted, despised and rejected of men. Can this be the meaning of that common portrayal of the prophet with the staff in his hand, that when you speak the truth, you had better be ready to travel? You have not called us to participate in any popularity contest or to be a candidate for "Man of the Year" or "Woman of the Year." You have called us to be bearers and declarers of truth. Help us to be aware at all times that Your message may alarm, even anger, if it is rightly proclaimed. Is it true, O Christ in heaven, that we have so muted Your message that hearers now listen to it as a baby listens to the lullaby? Have we been soothing when we should have been inflammatory, comforting when we should have been incitive? Is that why hostile people no longer seek to kill us? Is it true that we never find that which is worth living for until we find that which is worth dying for? Is it true that no longer is there danger in being Your disciple simply because we have so diluted and diminished Your Gospel as to minimize its demands — and minimized its promises? You have given Your answer in One Who thought it not robbery to be equal with God and Who still took upon himself the burden that rightly lay on the hearts of others and gave his life on the Cross. Praise be to You for the Answer, which we cannot ignore and dare not keep to ourselves! Amen.

* * * * *

(In his *Christian Discourses* SK writes: "The most important thing in life is to be in the correct position. This the Christian assumes in relation to the next day, for to him it is non-existent. It is well-known that in front of the actor, blinded as he is by the footlights, there is the deepest darkness, the blackest night. One might think that this would discompose him, render him uneasy. But no, ask him, and thou shalt hear him admit that this is precisely what gives him support, makes him calm, keeps him in the enchantment of deception. On the other hand, it would discompose him if he could see any single individual and catch a glimpse of an auditor. So it is with the next day. One sometimes complains and finds it tragic that the future is so dark before one. Ah, the misfortune is just this, that it is not dark enough when fear and presentiment and expectation and earthly impatience glimpse the next day! One who rows a boat turns his back to the goal towards which he labours. So it is with the next day. When by the help of eternity a man lives absorbed in today, he turns his back to the next day. The more he is eternally absorbed in today, the more decisively does he turn his back upon the next day, so that he does not see it at all. If he turns around, eternity is confused before his eyes, it becomes the next day. But if for the sake of labouring more effectually towards the goal (eternity) he turns his back, he does not see the next day at all, whereas by the help of eternity he sees quite clearly today and its task.")

Gracious Father, Your Son had told us to take no thought for tomorrow, and Your prophet has said, "Whatsoever your hand finds to do, do it with your might" — do it well and do it *now!* I want to concentrate on today and its duties. I want to be contemporary with myself! I don't want to be guilty of that all-prevalent sin, procrastination. You have given me today and since I do not know what a day may bring forth, I long to use it as a treasure; I long to invest it well. I know I must

> dream not too much of what I'll do tomorrow,
> Or how I'll live, perchance, another year.
> Tomorrow's chance I do not need to borrow:
> Today is here!

Guide me, so that in my impatience I do not neglect today and its demands and duties and thus miss eternity. Direct my thoughts, my moods, my actions toward that which is unseen and eternal. All this I ask in the name of Him Who is the same yesterday, today, and forever! Amen.

*   *   *   *   *

Chapter 12

Prayers For A
"Personalized Theology"
"What think Ye of Christ?"

(Like that of Augustine and of Luther, Kierkegaard's was a "personalized theology," a dynamic philosophy of the Christian life worked out in the agonizing struggles of his own soul. He felt a sense of guilt before God, a feeling of being "utterly undone." It was his belief that "each one of us must wrestle for himself with the vital problems of life which he himself had wrestled with, and which can only be solved in the individual life by actual living.")

Merciful God, we remember with fear and trembling the warning of your Blessed Apostle that at the last day everyone shall give account of himself before God. Fearful, indeed, is the realization that each one shall stand alone before Thy throne. There we cannot posture; we cannot pretend. We cannot come with any sense of pride in what we are or in what we have said or in what we have done. We know ourselves too well for that; we have inside information on how good or evil our lives have been. Even before that fateful day we acknowledge that there can be no peace and order in the world around us unless there is health and wholeness within. You did not put us here to tilt at wind-mills or to shadow-box. There are real enemies of Your purpose and Your will whom we must confront, and that confrontation begins in our own hearts.

Then when we stand at last before Thy throne of grace, we shall be thankful that it is the throne of *grace*, grace to cover all our sins. For we do not stand alone. Although my dearest brother cannot stand before You as my advocate, I do have One who "sticketh closer than a brother," and He is the Friend who lay down his life for me. Thank You, O Heavenly Father, for that Unspeakable Gift! Amen.

* * * * *

(As a child, SK was the object of ridicule and abuse from his peers and his playmates. As an adult, he was a victim of even harsher treatment on the part of friend and foe alike. Strangely, he accepted all this mental and moral abuse as a part of what it meant to be a true Christian. He would have none of the then-current preaching in the church to the effect that to the church member peace, prosperity, and happiness were a signed-sealed-and-delivered guarantee. On the contrary, he considered such a state of blessing as a sure sign of apostasy. Self-denial rather than self-gratification should be the sought-after goal of the true believer. Suffering is a gift of God to bring us close to the Suffering Saviour!)

O You Who are our Rock and Fortress, we often come to You out of a world where evil forces and evil people make life dangerous and threatening for all. Certainly these days of our lives have brought such forces and such people into play so that they affect the life of everyone. With the saint of old we cry, "Who shall deliver me from the wicked and unjust man?" We echo the plaint and the complaint of the Psalmist when he remonstrates with God that the evil prosper and are not in trouble as other men are. But in our hearts we know, O God, that when evil people cast long shadows, the sun is about to set and darkness is soon to follow. But to us who walk in darkness

You have given a Great Light, a Light that shines brightest when the darkness is deepest. That Light is Love, Love that is always at its best when bestowed on people at their worst. Grant, we pray, that we may walk ever in that Light. Amen.

* * * * *

(SK talks about the "magic mirror of possibility" before which many people preen themselves and in which they wish sometime to see reflections of their greatness. But for many it is only a wish and not a resolution or a plan. They may proclaim it loudly from the housetop as being their true intention when they should be working it out quietly in the secret work-room of the soul. "All of them have good intentions, and even resolutions and plans for life, yes, even for eternity. But the intention soon loses its youthful strength and fades away. The resolution is not firmly grounded and is unable to withstand opposition. It totters before circumstances and is altered by them." "Only a man of will," he says, "can be a true man of God.")

Thou God who *does* wonders, so much of what we call faith is nothing more than dreaming, day-dreaming with our eyes open to the enchanting image of what *might be,* but our powers remain suspended in a vacuum of indifference to the possibility of what *should become!* Father, we know the world's needs even as we ignore its demands.

> *Knowledge we ask not; knowledge*
> *Thou hast lent.*
> *But Lord, the* **will,** *there lies*
> *the bitter need.*
> *Give us to build above the*
> *deep intent*
> *The deed, the deed!*

105

We know that there are tasks that demand the firm grip of our hands, problems that need the immediate application of our minds, sorrows and trials that can only be eased when they are borne in our hearts. Use us, Lord as You will — and when and where. For Your Kingdom will be built only as obedient workers labor at it. Your will will be done only when able followers will that it be done. It is well to proclaim Your gospel from the housetops, but we must confess that we know we must come down to the dusty streets and filthy gutters to build in our midst that Kingdom which our housetop message proclaims. Guide us to where You want us and give us the will to do what You want done in spite of ourselves! Amen.

*   *   *   *   *

(At times it did appear that SK was self-contradictory in his philosophical stance as over against his religious beliefs. He held that "the mark of greatness is to be hated during one's lifetime." Yet he writes, "Adversity draws men together and produces beauty and harmony in life's relationships, just as the cold of winter produces ice-flowers on the window-pane which vanish with the warmth." He was submerged in adversity: his engagement to Regine, whom he loved and who loved him, was mysteriously terminated; his health, which was always precarious took a sudden and terminal turn for the worse; his father, with whom he had an ambivalent relationship oscillating between love and admiration on one hand and anger and hate on the other, died. Far from experiencing the warmth of harmony and sympathy in the midst of all this adversity, SK became the object of criticism, hostility, and condemnation from friends, and even from those who were his associates in the fraternity of the ordained. The one relationship that remained warm and strong was his relationship with God. As he became weaker and beleaguered, his one Rock and Fortress was the Father!)

O Father (if, indeed, we dare call Thee "Father"), there are times when we no longer feel that we are Thy children, times when it is hard to believe that we have been left so desolate and alone. We might be able to understand if we had done some grievous wrong or fallen before the onslaught of some dreadful temptation. Then, indeed, we would be receiving the just reward for our sins. But it is often when we have done nothing amiss that these overwhelming burdens fall upon us and the sense of being totally abandoned overcomes us. Family and friends seem so distant, so lacking in understanding, so completely uncaring. Give us the grace to remember, Heavenly Father, that we are not alone — You are with us. That assurance can melt the coldest frost on our spirits, turning the Winter of our discontent and our discomfort and our disenchantment into the budding Springtime of joy and peace and trust. What triumph! — to know that we are not alone, but we are in the company of Him Whose protecting care is all-providing and Whose Love is everlasting! Amen, and Amen!

* * * * *

(At times SK felt very uneasy about his calling as an ordained servant of God. He admitted that the medium through which God's pure, holy Word reaches the people is the clergy. "Now it is easy to see," he wrote, "that if this medium were quite without any selfishness, this would be perfection for then God's Word would reach the people for all practical purposes direct, the medium being no disturbance at all." It is not the prerogative of the messenger to change or alter the message. It is his sole — and his sacred — mission to deliver! Time and again there are those messengers who desire

107

to be critics, editors, and even authorities who, if they were willing to admit it, are moved to declare, not "Thus saith the Lord," but, "This is what *I* think!" O man of God, you are merely the trumpeter, there to sound the trumpet! But what often happens is what Paul sternly warned when he wrote, "If the trumpet gives an uncertain sound, who shall prepare himself for battle?")

Great Master, through Your Word You have given us our marching orders. Although those orders have been given direct to Your teachers and commanders, and when they are related to us by the firm, clear voices of Your messengers, we rise up eager for the march, reach to engage the enemy and lift Your holy banners high so that all the world will know Who is our Divine Commander and for whose cause we fight; yet when Your Word is not trumpeted clearly, correctly, we are "here as on a darkling plain swept with confused alarms of struggle and flight." Give us, O Lord, holy men of God, called to be true and dedicated to be true to that call! If Your Word is to be a lamp unto our feet and a light unto our path, then inspire them all to hold high that lamp in such a manner that neither the messenger nor the hand that holds it can be seen. In this way he shall know that You have spoken to us. We will know that the commands are true and righteous altogether, no matter where they lead or how fierce the struggle. Amen.

*   *   *   *   *

(SK charged that it was when their sacrosanct standing with people was lost and their authority was challenged that members of the clergy began to offer to the people a "watered-down Christianity." There was little choice for them but to loosen the cords of ecclesiastic discipline and tone down the demands of the Church. "And so they continued to water it down till in the end they achieved perfect conformity with an ordinary worldly run of ideas which were proclaimed Christian. That is more or less what Protestantism is now.")

Eternal God, You Who are absolute Truth, absolute Righteousness, absolute Holiness, we find ourselves of a sudden in the midst of an age of convenience, compromise, accommodation. It is all right to be charitable — if it does not cost too much; good to be forgiving — if it does not place you at a disadvantage; fine to sacrifice — up to a point! But then, we encounter Your Son Who speaks of "going the second mile," of "doing more than others," of not even letting the right hand know what the left hand is doing. Those things He said: "Love your enemies; do good to them that hate you; pray for them who despitefully use you and persecute you" — sometimes I wonder if those things are not impossible. But then I see Him in the Garden, before Pilate, on the Cross and I wonder: Is anything else possible? O make this impossible possibility possible in me! Amen.

*　*　*　*　*

(SK made no secret of the fact that he loved the writings of Meister Eckhart and all that the great saint represented. When anyone spoke of the dangers of discipleship (and there are many!), or about the need for spiritual courage in that day (and it is desperately needed in every age!), SK was quick to quote the intrepid follower of Jesus, for Meister Eckhart declared, "There are plenty to follow our Lord halfway, but not the other half! You cannot be half-and-half." Whoever is not *for* the Lord, whole-heartedly so, is *against* Him. Whoever does not willingly and cheerfully go the second mile has wasted his energies by going the first. Christian swimmers try to keep one foot on the bottom when they should be willing to "plunge in 70,000 fathoms deep where life depends not upon half measures but upon faith.")

Lord, You have warned us that we cannot serve two masters. But in our day we have tried to serve many masters, and we have a difficult time determining each one's place in our pantheon. Your demands are not too great, especially since obedience to them brings the greatest and most lasting blessings that life and love can give. Forgive us for merely expressing admiration for those who labor and sacrifice, but feel no desire to emulate them. Forgive us for the concealed, but apparent, desire to be "carried to the skies on flowery beds of ease." Forgive us if, when the gauntlet is laid down, we hide in cringing fear behind closed doors as Your followers did long ago. But guide us, behind those doors, to pray as did they for Your Holy Spirit to fill us with that same power that enabled them to launch out with newly-given zeal, going everywhere and preaching with boldness Your Word. Amen.

*   *   *   *   *

(In *The Present Age* Kierkegaard writes that the one who prays has the mistaken idea that the most important thing about his prayer is that God hear it and heed it. Yet, the exact opposite of that is true. True success in prayer is not "that *God hears* what is prayed for, but that the person praying continues to pray until *he is the one who hears* and thus knows what God wants and what God wills." The real difference is between "spate" and "wait." Instead of "waiting on the Lord," the pray-er pours out a "spate" of demands and complaints and wearies the heart of a Father Who longs to speak to His child!)

O waiting Father, we confess that at times we are so urgent in our praying that we pummel you with our wordy assaults, thinking, as did the importunate widow, that we will be heard for our much speaking. Teach us that You do not deal in the numbers game; we will not be heard for our endless, and often mindless, jabber. One word from a needy, pleading heart carries more weight with You than an encyclopedic outpouring of everything that is in our troubled minds. How impertinent and imperious we are that we feel the need to tell You, the Omniscient, what You already know! Make us humble enough to acknowledge that You have more to impart to us than we have to impart to You. May we who shout to get the world's attention learn to wait in quietness and trust for the whisper of Your still, small Voice. Amen.

* * * * *

(How imperative it is to possess a fair and equitable assessment of your own worth. It does much for your self-esteem. But you do not get a true picture from self-appraisal nor from the judgment of others. SK reveals to us his standard of measurement: "It is necessary to know oneself. For he who does not know himself cannot recognize himself either, and we can never recognize ourselves except inasmuch as we know ourselves. Thus, there has to be some preparation. Materially also — when a man accidentally happens to see himself in a mirror, or when the mirror is so placed that he does not know that the image seen is a reflection of the mirror and that the reflection is himself — it happens that we do not recognize ourselves. Paganism required: know yourself. Christianity answers: no, this 'know yourself' is a preliminary. Then look at yourself in the mirror of the Word to really know yourself. There is no true knowledge of self without knowledge of God, or without being before God. To be in front of the mirror is to be in front of God.")

O God of the meek and lowly, how eagerly we seek to see ourselves as others see us! How solicitous we are that humankind might think highly of us! But how much more eager we are to merit Your approbation and acclaim! Yet, when we glance into the mirror of Your Word, we are humbled, yea, even horrified by what we see there. Our lives fall so short of the goodness and the grandeur of even inanimate things. Your mountains are more majestic than we can ever be. The rippling mountain streams gurgle with a sparkling purity that only accentuates the defilement in our lives. The flowers and the fields exude a beauty that is pristine and holy, whereas our lives, we confess, are tarnished and dull with the clingings of a self that is too much with us. If only our speech were as harmless and sweet as that of the birds' songs! If only our care for our young approached the instinctive care of the fowls of the air and the animals of the field! When I consider the heavens, they do, indeed, reveal the touch of Thy Fingers, where it would seem at times that not You, O God, but Satan, was our creator. And then — the sun, the moon, and the stars, so lofty, so noble, so shining — while we live lives that are dull and lustreless. But then, then I turn to Your Word, O Lord: "When I look at thy heavens, the work of thy fingers, the moon and the stars which thou hast established, what is man that thou art mindful of him, and the son of man that thou dost care for him? Yet thou hast made him little less than God, and dost crown him with glory and honor." Simple are the words and even the thought of the age-old nursery rhyme, but what comfort it brings to the soul:

> *O great, wide, wonderful, beautiful world,*
> *With the silvery waters around you curled*
> *And the grass upon your breast!*
> *World, you are beautifully dressed.*
> *Yet, when I knelt to say my prayers today,*
> *A voice inside me seemed to say:*
> *"You are greater than the world*
> *Though you are such a tiny dot,*
> *For you can love and think and the world cannot!"*

How You can think so much of me and yet be the great and mighty and pure and holy God that You are may be darkness to my intellect, but it truly is sunshine to my heart! Amen.

* * * * *

("God is the Examiner," writes SK, and he goes on to say, "This is a highly significant term. An examiner, in short, really has nothing in common with someone who, humanly speaking, has a cause. But, to be sure, in this era of phraseology, all concepts have been turned inside out, and we finally have no word to designate what elevation is. Nowadays, a school teacher means someone who needs children, doctor someone who needs the sick, and professor someone who needs disciples. So undoubtedly also, examiner means someone who needs candidates for examination." The inference is, of course, that God, the Examiner, needs people so that He has someone to examine!)

O Divine Examiner, we fill our world with a multitude of things that entrance us and entice us. Even our own hearts bewilder and betray us at times. Specious invitations and promised pleasantries lull our consciences to sleep and lead us far astray. Like the proverbial greyhound that became a lowly dachshund because he wore down his legs chasing a lifeless rabbit, so we dissipate our powers by our relentless pursuit of that which is no gain even when we catch it! And the promise of Your Word is true: eventually our sins will find us out. When they do disclose our guilt and unmask our pretense, we cry out against the heavens. Just as there are those who shout and then command the echoes not to disturb them, so we sin and then irately resent the inevitable consequences of our wickedness and our wrongdoing. O Lord, with sorrow and with shame "before Thee we confess how little we who own Thy Name, Thy mind, Thy ways express!" Is it You, the Examiner,

Who needs us simply because You must have sinners to examine and judge? We need You more than You need us. Search me, O God, and test my weaknesses and find if there be any wicked way in me. Even though You find wicked ways in me, lead me in the Way Everlasting. Amen.

*   *   *   *   *

Chapter 13

Prayers Against
"Protective Abstraction"
"I know whom I have believed!"

(Deploring the enervating faintheartedness of those in public life, SK pointed out that politicians and clergy alike were guilty of spiritual cowardice and were misleading their people into the same disgraceful weaknesses. "What men desire is a protective abstraction, by means of which a person can avoid being I, that being the most destructive and disastrous state imaginable." The politician says, "This is what *the public* demands." The cleric says, "This is the view that *the Church* takes." Thus, they hide behind the cloak of anonymity, taking no onerous responsibility and assuming no courageous stance. SK contends that the "basic corruption of our time" is the abolition of personal responsibility and accountability. It is a fundamental peril to any age.)

O Master, even as Your brave apostle Paul wrote to Timothy, You have saved us and called us with a holy calling not to be mere echoes, but to be Your preacher, Your apostle, Your teacher. You have called us to stand before the common people and kings and proclaim, "I have heard His Word, I have experienced His love, and now I declare this unto you!" I do confess that often, in the face of challenge and opposition, I become a wavering, quavering disciple, slinking in the shadows, following, but following from afar. To be sure, never do I claim that I do not know You, but by my indecisive hesitancy I convey that disgraceful impression that You are only a casual acquaintance. Can it be, O Lord, that you desire and need *my* witness, *my* testimony, *my* discipleship? Yea, down through the corridors of the ages reverberates the question: "What think *ye* of Christ, when all's said and done?" Lord, I do not need the protective anonymity of the mob. Standing alone, under stormy skies and confronting hostile assailants, let my voice ring out, though it be the only voice that can be heard, "Thou art the Christ, *my* Lord and *my* God!" Amen.

* * * * *

(If many a man were asked, "What is your highest desire? What do you really want in Life?" — the honest answer would be, "I want everything!" When Jesus visited the home of Mary and Martha and Mary sat listening to Him while Martha prepared the meal, Jesus said that Mary had chosen the "better part." SK asked, "What is the better part? It is God, and consequently everything. The better part is everything but it is called the better part because it must be chosen; one does not receive everything as everything; that is not how one begins, one begins by choosing the better part, which is, nevertheless, everything.")

God of Abraham, and of Isaac, and of Jacob, at the very entrance to the Promised Land You challenged Your servant with a choice: "Choose you this day whom you will serve; whether the gods which your fathers served that were on the other side of the flood, or the gods of the Amorites, in whose land you dwell." When Joshua chose to serve the Lord, the door was closed to any other god. Choosing closes the door on the unchosen. All that is left is what has been chosen, and that is everything from that moment on. We have heard Your joyful

116

challenge and have made the joyful choice: "As for me and my house, we will serve the Lord!" Open for us the very sluice-gates of heaven to pour down Your blessings, for eye has not seen, ear has not heard, neither have entered into the minds of men the things that You have prepared for those who love you. You have given Your answer, and it is "everything!" Thanks be unto You, O God, for Your immeasurable bounty! Amen.

*   *   *   *   *

(For a time after breaking his engagement to Regine Olsen, whom he loved, SK was smitten with remorse, feeling that he had wronged the girl. He was tempted to move out of the country in order that he would not be constantly confronted by reminders of his actions. But he concluded, "I could go far away, live in a foreign country, a new life far from the memory, far from every possibility of its being revealed. I could live a hidden, secret life — but No, I must remain where I am and continue life as usual, without a single prudential measure, leaving everything to God.")

Often, O God, I have been tempted to flee from where I am, thinking to rid myself of the spectre of wrongs I have committed and the good I have left undone. But deep in my heart I know that I am seeking only to flee from myself, for even as my virtues are a part of me, so my sins are also a part of me. In the midnight of my sorrow I seek to drown my morbid moroseness in drink and drugs in order to get away from this, my sinful self, but morning comes and I am back with self on awakening — and it is a less compatible, less capable self that I must deal with the next day. Of a sudden, O merciful Father, I am aware that this weak and sinful self need not stagger under the deadening and deadly weight of sins. You have taken them all away and nailed them to the Cross. Now I

117

can accept what I am and where I am because You have changed both. Praise the Lord, O my soul, and bless His Holy Name! Amen.

* * * * *

(Why is it that man seeks to change his location and his situation when things go badly for him? SK pondered that question in his own misfortune. He concluded that such a change for him would not entail a long, long journey. "It is only a step," he writes, "only a single step, a decisive step, and you have emigrated, for the Eternal lies much nearer to you than any foreign country to the emigrant, and yet when you are there, the change is infinitely great. So then, go with God to God, always take that one step more, that single step that even you, who cannot move a limb, are still able to take.")

O Thou Who art my Rock and my Fortress, how often have I found myself in the midst of sorrows that I cannot comfort, wrongs that I cannot right, burdens that I cannot carry, and evils that I cannot change. I turn this way and that, to one person and then another, to some strong nostrum and then a stronger! O God, where shall I find help? If I even take the wings of the morning and dwell in the uttermost parts of the earth or the sea, even there my troubles follow me and my sorrows and sins inundate my soul. Wretched man that I am! — who can deliver my soul? Out of the dim distant ages echoes the cry of the Psalmist: "From the end of the earth will I cry unto Thee, when my heart is overwhelmed: lead me to the rock that is higher than I." You *are* my Rock and my Fortress, then, O God, my very present Help in trouble. Help me, too, to go with God to God! Amen.

* * * * *

(SK could have had our own generation in mind when he wrote: "The result of human progress is that everything becomes thinner and thinner — the result of divine providence is to make everything inward." Modern progress is measured by the abundance of *things* that can be added to life, things that afford luxury, comfort, convenience. Occasionally it occurs to our benumbed sensibilities that it is not material things that count, but spiritual powers. SK added, "There are insects which defend themselves against their enemies by raising dust. So man himself seeks to defend himself against the idea and against spirit by raising numbers. Man as an animal is related directly to numbers, it is numbers he believes in.")

O God of the poor, to whom You offer eternal riches, humbly we confess that we are all tempted to seek more and more, but more and more becomes less and less when we allow ourselves to be suffocated by the abundance of things we possess. The important things in life *are not things!* — unless we are content to live insect lives and raise the dust of indistinction between the good and the evil, between the temporary and the eternal. The more we love and cherish the material, the less affection and desire we have for the spiritual. And You have not created us to grovel among trifles or to gorge ourselves on the garbage when we might enjoy the feast. You have not made us to crawl when we might soar! Henceforth, give us grace and wisdom to seek those things that are above, through Christ Who is at Your right Hand. Amen.

* * * * *

(Kierkegaard often shocked his brothers in the ordained ministry by his portrayal of what he believed to be the nature of Christianity and the traits of the true believer. And no more so than when

119

he spoke of "the scandal" of Christianity. A "joy-less" faith is an insult to God in his view. He writes, "Properly understood, every man who truthfully desires a relation to God and to live in his sight has only one task: always to be joyful!" As long as I merely *discuss* doctrine "and indulge my cleverness or profundity or my eloquence or my imaginative power in depicting it: the people are pleased. But the moment I begin to express existentially what I say, and consequently to bring this Christian faith into reality; it is just as though I had exploded existence — the scandal is there at once.")

Gracious and understanding Master of us all, we believe, indeed, that the presence of our Lord is always a greater power for joy in our life than the forces of Satan are for sorrow. Is it a scandal to live triumphantly in the very face of the Enemy, to exude joy in the presence of evil and trouble? All the wickedness and sadness in this universe is no match for our "joy in the Lord." "Rejoice in the Lord always," Paul writes in his letter to the Church at Philippi, and no wonder it is called the "epistle of joy" — Christ is mentioned more than 50 times in those four brief chapters. Anyone who is constantly and conscientiously aware and mindful of his Lord is bound to be joyful! The faith You have bestowed upon us was not meant to be a soporific to the heart or an aphrodisiac to the mind. It is The Way — The Way Christ lived, The Way Christ taught, the Way that He would have us walk, and that Way is The Way of inextinguishable, inexhaustible joy! No matter how brief or how long the journey, no matter how rich or poor our circumstances, no matter how burdensome or easy the load, no matter how smooth or rough the way — let us walk that way, rejoicing in Him Who is the joy of every loving heart! Amen.

* * * * *

(God understands us when no one and nothing else does. That is the reason that communion with nature is not enough; we need communion with God. He who seeks solace and help in nature alone, as some are mindful to do, finds neither solace nor guidance. To be sure, the very stars in their courses became the allies of God's people as they fought against Sisera long ago. But nature disregards the lost wanderer, SK contends. "The stars are so far away that they cannot see the wanderer. It is only the wanderer who can see the stars, hence there is no communion between him and the stars." The murmuring brook may lull the lost one to sleep but it cannot point out the way to him. "The brook goes on murmuring, and the wanderer at its side grows older." But He Who is the Omniscient One "knows our every thought from a distance, knows plainly the path of each thought, even when it eludes man's own consciousness. He is an Omniscient One who seeth in secret, with Whom man speaks even in silence, so that no one shall venture to deceive Him either by talk, or by silence, as in this world where one man can conceal much from the other now by being silent, and again even more by talking.")

O God, to Whom all hearts are open and from Whom no secrets are hid, although all the universe above me and all the people around me with whom I press elbows daily do not understand me, are often not even aware of me, it fortifies my soul to know that there is One to Whom I can turn, One on Whom I can lean. Oh, I could pour out my woes to the deep, mysterious forests, or proclaim my sins to the very mountains, or express my adoration to the sunset. But the forests would remain dark and forbidding; the mountains would merely echo my confessions, revealing my secrets to all the world; the sunset would fade with never a flickering response to my adoration.

There is no answer from them because they have no answer to give. And I long to *commune*, not merely *complain* and *confess*. I long to be able to listen to a Voice, not just be annoyed by the woeful echo of my own voice. You have created us for companionship, Our Creator, in order that You might claim the love of all whom You have made — *and* that all whom You have made might claim the support and the joy of Your Presence. Because we know You will answer, we ask that You give us courage to be radiant when all goes against us, for in such radiance we glorify You more than in hours of prosperity, even as the lighted candle casts more radiance in the darkness than it ever can at noonday. Let us be lights, shining in dark places, until the radiance of Christ Himself dawns upon benighted souls, leading them into light. Amen.

*   *   *   *   *

(From whence do our ideas and our ideals come? In his dealing with "the meaning of my existence in the present time," SK writes: "In the same way that other men travel abroad and then bring home news of the habits and customs of foreign countries — I too have lived abroad for many years in the company of ideals where it is such happiness to be, where everything is gentle and mild, if only one is unassuming and humble." He who knows that his "citizenship is in heaven" need never leave home in order to know and cherish the ideas and ideals of that "other country." He can make those ideas and those ideals come alive where he dwells so that they supersede the law and outdate the worn customs of that land in which is he merely a temporary dweller!)

O You Who are the Friend of every stranger and sojourner who roams this tangled jungle that we call "the world," let us never forget who we are and Whose we are. We are in the world but not of it. Our citizenship *is* in heaven. You have set us down in a world of darkness, but in that darkness You have called us to walk in the light and to walk as children of light. Even as You called Your people out of Egypt long ago, so You have called us out of slavery to the lowly demands of the flesh in order that we might offer ourselves as servants to Him Who claims the heart. You have placed us in the company of strutting, but stumbling, people who ridicule our claim to any but earthly citizenship and who seek to tempt us with the frivolous baubles of the lowly realm that they have chosen. But the titillating sights and the seducing sounds of this worldly setting do not compare with the glimpses You have imparted to us of an invisible glory. We believe and affirm that eye has not seen, ear has not heard, neither have entered into the thoughts of man the things that You have prepared for those who love You and for those whom You love! When we are tempted to wander inquisitively down the inviting paths of the ways of the world, we are forsaking our heavenly citizenship and the company of the redeemed and are following the clamor of the crowd. We praise You, our Ruler and King, that we do not need to go along with the crowd. We do not need to order our footsteps according to the mundane regulations and restrictions of man's law when we can live by the high and noble truths of God. We praise You that we need not go along with the crowd because we walk in the company of One Who makes us stronger than the crowd. We praise You that this world is, truly, a bridge and we can pass over without building for ourselves any permanent abiding-place. Amen.

* * * * *

(SK deplores "low-pressure Christianity," a trend that would reduce the Christian faith to the lowest common denominator and thus produce what he refers to as "battalions of mediocrity." He condemns the apostle Peter as "an apostle of mediocrity" when that disciple remonstrates with Jesus

123

as his Master prepares to make his last visit to
Jerusalem and go *all the way* in his ministry — even
unto death. For Peter "to try to dissuade his teacher
and friend from voluntarily exposing himself to
death is infamy, it is the suggestion of Satan. Nothing more is needed to see that the kind of level-
ling which is Christendom is neither more nor less
than disgrace, the work of Satan, and all our mediocre Christian teachers are nothing more than a
shame and Satan's instruments.")

O Matchless Master, You have called us to do "more than
others," to "go the second mile" and the third and fouth, and
farther — even unto death. Let no trace of mediocrity infest
the temper or infect the temperature of our behavior. Make
our devotion to be a steady and a steadfast loyalty, not moved
by every wind that blows, whether that wind be generated by
friend or foe. When misfortune comes our way, let us not be
troubled when those more fortunate than we, though unbeliev-
ing, mock and ridicule us for our trust in You. Give us the
power and the will to reject all worldly standards as the gauge
of our faith and to look for the things that are unseen and
eternal. Thus, we shall give to all vicissitudes of life the stamp
of Christian courage and trust. One day, we know, You will
give your blessed stamp of loving approval and joy in Your
people. How easy it is to be mediocre — easy and useless! How
difficult it is to live for the things that are excellent — but not
difficult with Thy help! O Christ of the unspeakable and perfect way, strengthen us to walk in that Way! Amen.

*   *   *   *   *

(In judging the preaching current in his day SK
regretted that during the early period of a man's
career "the greatest danger is *not to take the risk*"
because "by not risking at first one turns aside and
serves trivialities." He felt that Bishop Mynster,

124

his own and his father's priest and friend, demeaned the gospel by his lukewarm witness and his fear of alienating his hearers. On Whitsunday in 1850 (May 19) SK entered into his *Journal:* "Today Mynster preached against monks and hermits — Good God, to want to play that tune in the 19th century in order to be rewarded with applause. He did not attack a single one of the forms of evil prevalent in our day — ugh, God forbid, that might easily have become all too serious, no, he preached against — the monasteries!")

Lord, to You Who risked all we pray. But we hesitate to be too daring, even in our prayers, for we have not risked much that we have or much that we are. There are times when we strike out daringly, like Peter when Jesus came to the disciples walking on the water. Some of us are in favored and favorite circumstances, Lord. We have much to lose. Although we desire to come to You, stormy sea or calm, we cannot walk on the water unless we are willing to get out of the boat. But we don't want to leave the boat — or *rock* the boat, either. Guard us against preaching inanities when there are vital and viable issues to be faced. Forgive us for preoccupation with mists and dews when our people are under deep clouds of sorrow and need or are even submerged by the storms and the tempests of outrageous fortune. Give us the courage to be the kind of individual who is ready and willing that God speak through him, who "in spite of the stares of the wise, and the world's derision, dares to travel the star-blazed trail, dares to follow the vision" in the Name of One Who did not count the cost. Amen.

*　*　*　*　*

Chapter 14

Prayers For
Eternal Vigilance

*"Watch and pray, for you
know neither the day nor the
hour when the Lord shall come."*

(Faith involves an ever-living, never-ceasing vigor and vigilance. To SK it was never a destination that had been reached or a proposition that had been settled. He writes: "It is perfectly true, as philosophers say, that life must be understood backwards. But they forget the other proposition, that it must be lived forwards. And if one thinks over that proposition it becomes more and more evident that life can never really be understood in time simply because at no particular moment can I find the necessary resting-place from which to understand it." One of his contemporary philosophers with whom SK could agree was Baron von Hugel who stated that "no amount of *ought-ness* will ever take the place of *is-ness.*" "I will not grieve over the past," writes SK, "for why grieve? I will work on with energy and not waste time grieving, like the man caught in the quicksands who began calculating how far down he had already sunk, forgetting that all the while he was sinking still deeper." He cautions against getting stuck in the "mudbank of reason," because "the highest is not to understand the highest but to act on it.")

Eternal God, there are mudbanks and quicksands along every path that the pilgrim takes as he travels the highways and byways of this earthly journey. We live and move and have our being in the very midst of sorrows that have clogged the way for many, sufferings that have never been explained, wrongs that have never been made right, troubles that have never been alleviated. But "forgetting what lies behind and straining forward to what lies ahead, we press on toward the prize of the upward call of God in Christ Jesus." While the philosopher hems and haws and hammers and saws at his reconstruction of what "might have been," give us grace to press on to what ought to be and what, by Thy grace, O God, can be! You have not declared any moratorium on Your promises. In Your Word what endless glory shines! Make some of that glory shine in us as we meditate and cherish that Word so that Your radiance, through us, may light the way for others. Amen.

*　*　*　*　*

(There is a vast difference between attending a theatre to witness a dramatic or musical presentation and, on the other hand, attending a church where people are gathered together to engage in worship. At the theatre members of the audience are all spectators, liking or disliking the program, passing judgment on every phase of it. Every member of the theatre audience is a critic and indulges heatedly and whole-heartedly in that criticism. Such is not the case in the church when the congregation worships. There are no spectators, only participants. The only one looking on is God Himself, and He judges how we worship if, indeed, we worship at all. Some may presume to pass judgment on the music, the preaching, and the attitude of other worshipers. But, as SK contends, "God's presence is the decisive thing that changes all. As soon as God is present, each man in the presence of God has the task of paying attention to himself.

128

The speaker must see that during the address he pays attention to himself, to what he says; the listener, that during the address he pays attention to himself, to how he listens, and whether during the address he, in his inner self, secretly talks with God. If this were not done, then the listeners would be presuming to share God's task with him.")

O You Who are the lover of the just and the unjust, when I flee to Your place of worship, I am approaching the divine mercy-seat and within that hallowed place I am meeting with my Lord. Tempted as I am to pass human judgment on all that I witness there, remind me that my presence there is not as critic or even as silent impartial observer. I am there as one of Your Family, joining others of the Household of Faith in praise and prayer — and in penitence! Forgive me for assuming the spectator role where there are no spectators permitted. How another may come to You and what he bears in his heart is not mine to question or to judge. Sufficient is the charge that weighs upon my own heart! How can I pass judgment on my fellow-worshiper when I falter under my own shortcomings? How can I fault this one or that one for coming ill-prepared and undeserving when my own approach is shabby and inept? How can I measure the degree of another's sincerity and humility when that very act would disclose my own pride and hypocrisy? I come, not boasting any merit of my own, only seeking answers and help in my need. You, O God, are the Fountain of Hope, and I thirst. Let me drink of Your living waters. You are the Treasure-House of all that is high and noble, and I am poor and lowly. Feed me with the riches of Your grace. You are the Feast of mercy and love, and I hunger. Let me partake of the kind of food which means that I will never hunger again. You are the Rock on which the wise can build. My whole being trembles and totters. Be the strong Foundation that will enable my life to stand forever! As we look, not to others or at others, but only to our Lord, open Your holy Bible to our hearts and our hearts to the holy Bible,

there to behold the wonder of Your Presence and Your Promise
— and thus, together, partake of both! In the name of Him
Who came not to condemn, but to save! Amen.

*　*　*　*　*

(SK did not hesitate to express his contempt for
the manner in which the Denmark Church sought
to promulgate a kind of Christendom that was far
removed from New Testament Christianity. The
priests gave more attention to their own comforts,
luxuries, and prestige than they did to the needs
of people who dwelt within the very shadow of the
Church. "All this," he wrote wryly, "in a society
where everyone is Christian; where there are a
thousand sworn pastors, of whom — yes, it is true
that it is only for three-quarters of an hour on Sun-
days that the majority of people learn from these
men that Christianity is the renunciation of the
earthly and putting God first; for the rest of the
Sunday, and for the whole of the week, they learn
from these men, especially by their example [and
example has, as is well-known, a quite different effect from words], that Christianity and the serious-
ness of life mean to strive for the earthly, and for
their own selfish desires." Moreover, their people
are led into the same pitfalls that snare the priests,
for "those who have some time left for religion all
wish to settle it as early or as quickly as possible
— that they too may get busy enjoying this life.
So perhaps they have a moment left over, now and
then, for religion; but on condition that it becomes
a kind of enjoyment, and that it is settled once for
all that they have religion, so that they are sure
of the blessedness of eternity.")

Merciful God, as it happens in every age, so in our age the
Church faces the danger of becoming nothing more than a

stained-glass jungle where the members snap and snarl and growl at one another because they do not realize how much they need each other and how much others need them. Even as it is true that the individual cannot break down when he is helping another up, so the Church will not falter or fail so long as it is dedicated to steadying those who falter and seek success for those who fail. You have blessed us so that we can be a blessing; You have strengthened us in order that we can impart strength; You have enriched our lives so that wherever Your Church reaches through us, there no one need live in poverty any longer. We realize that challenges are great, that obstacles are formidable. But now, as never before, we pray that You will make Your people equal to the task; that You will empower Your Church in order that it may be a power; that You will impart to us the "joy of the Lord" as we seek to transmit joy into those lives where neither the sun of the heavens nor the Son of Righteousness any longer shines. You have not ordained Your Church to remain "spacious, splendid, and empty." If Your people are full of the joy of the Lord, that joy will become a treasure of all people everywhere, for our souls will be too filled with that joy to contain it. The overflow will spill into the world around us and so enfold the disinherited, the discredited, the disillusioned, and even the disgraced that they will know God cares — all because we care! Make Thy Church, dear Saviour, "a lamp of burnished gold to hold before the nations Thy true light as of old!" Amen.

* * * * *

(SK amazed and often stunned his peers by many of his statements. But he astounds the ages by his contention, quoted elsewhere, that in his relation to God man has only one duty: "always to be joyful." This was written in his *Journal* in 1847, some years after his father died, one year after the public attacks on him in *Corsair,* and the very year in which Regine, to whom he had been engaged,

131

married Friedrich Schlegel. How could one who has been known through the years as "the melancholy Dane" possibly say that? His bitter childhood memories, his physical limitations, his broken engagement, his alienation from his family, his break with the established Church, all would seem to suggest that joy was the furthest thing from his mind. But a later entry in his *Journal* gives what is undoubtedly the reason for his joy: "In melancholy sympathy, though myself unhappy, I loved men and the mass of men. Their bestial conduct towards me compelled me, in order to endure it, to have more and more to do with God." So, friendless, he found a Friend in God; love-lorn, he found love in the Lord.)

God is love. If I am to have more and more to do with You, O God, I must remember that You are love. Love covers a multitude of sins, and I have more than a multitude of sins to be covered. Love is greatest when bestowed upon the one least deserving of love, and I am unceasingly aware of Great Love, the Greatest! Our Master, "having loved His own, He loved them to the end," and "His own" are the unloved and the unlovely, those whom the world rejected and rejects. Though poor, He makes all rich; though lowly, yea, the lowliest of the lowly, a servant, He lifts up the lowest and makes them to walk in high places. And it is all because He was "touched by the feeling of our infirmities." And me? — How unfeeling and how untouched with the cares and the sorrows and the needs of others I often am! Again and again I have been brought up short by my lack of compassion. "Don't let the misery and needs of others cause you to lose sleep" I have told myself. How often have I dismissed my duty and obligations to the down-and-out by saying to myself and even to others, "They have made their bed, let them lie in it." But that very thought brings to mind the words of Him who said to the helpless, "Rise, take up thy bed and walk!" Sensitize my heart to the stranger, the poor, the hungry, the thirsty, the naked, those sick and in prison. Teach me that if I am to have more and more to do with Thee, I must do more and more for *these!* Amen.

* * * * *

(Kierkegaard quotes Aristotle who says that philosophy begins with wonder not as in our day with doubt. And wonder need not depend on reason or reasons, on understanding and congealed certainties. "For the rights of understanding to be valid one must venture out into life, out on the sea and lift up one's voice even though God hears it not, and not to stand on the shore and watch others fighting and struggling — only then does understanding acquire its *official sanction,* for to stand on one leg and prove God's presence is a very different thing from going on one's knees and thanking Him." SK claims the problem is not to understand Christianity, but to understand that it cannot be understood. Again he writes, "Until now people have always expressed themselves in the following way: the knowledge that one cannot understand this or the other thing is the mistake; people ought to say the very opposite: if human science refuses to understand that there is something which it cannot understand, or better still, that there is something about which it clearly understands that it cannot understand it — then all is confusion. For it is the duty of the human understanding to understand that there are things which it cannot understand.")

Almighty and All-Knowing God, even if my reason were able to stand on two legs or, like the millipede on a thousand legs, there are mysteries before which I bow my knees daily, neither presuming to know nor rebelling because greater knowledge is denied me. I need not hear the long catalogue of phenomena, perplexities, and problems that have bewildered the mind of man through the ages. It is enough, O Lord, that I am confronted and confused by a multitude of mysteries in my own experience in my own day.

> *I cannot understand the why or wherefore*
> *   of a thousand things*
> *The burdens, the annoyances, the*
> *   daily stings;*
> *I cannot understand, but I can trust,*
> *And perfect trusting perfect comfort*
> *   brings.*
> *I cannot see the end, the hidden meaning*
> *   of each trial sent,*
> *The pattern into which each tangled thread is bent;*
> *I cannot see the end, but I can trust.*
> *And in God's changeless love I am content.*

You have given me a marvelous mind and reason whereby I can, indeed, unravel many daily mysteries and even begin to count the constellations and the stars. But by Your grace I am reminded that I can only *begin* to count. The glories of this universe are more and more, and I know less and less about those glories the more I know! Yet, increase my wisdom and my judgment, O God, as my knowledge increases. Above all, increase in my heart the love and devotion to You, without which all my knowledge is ignorance. Amen.

* * * * *

(SK had an unusual answer to give to those who wondered why he never prayed to be delivered from suffering. In 1853 he wrote in his *Journal:* "There was a time — it came so naturally, it was childlike — when I believed that God's love also expressed itself by sending earthly 'good gifts,'

134

happiness, prosperity. How foolhardy my soul was in desiring, and daring — for this is how I thought of it: one must not make the all-powerful petty; I prayed for everything, even the most foolhardy things, yet one thing expected, exemption from the deep suffering beneath which I have suffered from my earliest days, but which I understood as belonging to my relation to God." Somehow he felt that there was some purpose in suffering, even when he could not see it. He continues: "Little by little I noticed increasingly that all those whom God really loved had all had to suffer in this world. Furthermore, that that is the teaching of Christianity: to be loved by God and to love God is to suffer."

God of mercies, even as man has struggled through the ages, so we struggle even yet with this annihilating problem, suffering. We call on You in the daytime and in the night we are not silent but — no answer! Since we cannot snatch our answer from the unresponsive glowering heavens or come upon it in the shadows of the night when it troubles us most, we can only turn to Your Word, which is to be a lamp unto our feet and a light unto our path. There we come upon a man who was ever aware of a painful thorn in the flesh but who resolved "that I may gain Christ ... that I may know him and the power of his resurrection, and may share his sufferings, becoming like him in death, that if possible, I may attain the resurrection from the dead." Christ is pleading with me, then, to relate my sufferings directly to his sufferings, to know Him in the fellowship of sufferers. Somehow we sense that relating ourselves to Him in all things, and especially in suffering, we thus partake of his divine power. Not release and relief from suffering, then, we pray for, O God, but for the power that comes through our closeness to Him in all things. Time after time, because I have departed far from Him, I suffer since my ills are self-inflicted and there is only self to blame. When then? Help us to accept the suffering, not as punishment but as a guiding light, *warning* light, which flashes in the soul, and painfully we are reminded of Your love. If I love You, O God, it is more urgent that I suffer rather than that I cease to love. O precious pain, O merciful misery, that bring us close to Thee. Amen.

*   *   *   *   *

(Kierkegaard realized that men resign themselves to the coming of old age and often resent it to the degree that they wish life were all over. But he felt that in doing so they imperiled God's purposes for them and thus did not fully fulfil in life the mission entrusted to them. "It is very dangerous," he contended, "to go into eternity with possibilities which one has oneself prevented from becoming realities. A possibility is a hint from God. One must follow it. In every man there is latent the highest possibility; one must follow it. If God does not wish it then let Him prevent it, but one must not hinder oneself. Trusting to God I have dared, but I was not successful; in that is to be found peace, calm, and confidence in God. I have not dared, that is a woeful thought, a torment in eternity." We must live in expectation of, and in *anticipation* of, the fulfillment of life's promise, no matter how long we have to wait. "The Lord comes, even though we have to wait for him, he comes even though we grow as old as Anna, as grey as Simeon.")

God of the aged and the ageless! How often have we taken offense, how often have we resented it, those words that the young so glibly quote:

Grow old along with me!
The best is yet to be,
The last of life for which
*   the first was made.*

136

Many, when they do grow old, make a disturbing discovery. They discover that that "best that is yet to be" is fraught with debility, pain, separation from loved ones, and general miseries too numerous to mention. God of the aged, Your people confess that advancing age brings upon them a feeling of futility, a despondent suspicion that they are stringing beads on a string that has no knot in it! And it is exactly that, O Lord, if we count You out, but not, mind You, if we count You in. We have not fulfilled Your wish for us, Your divine purpose, unless we go through life, *all* of it, under full sail! "The best is yet to be?" We have not heard or seen it all, even as we tend to overlook the complete word of the poet, for he revealed the *whole* truth:

> *Grow old along with me!*
> *The best is yet to be,*
> *The last of life for which the first was made.*
> *Our times are in His hand*
> *Who saith, "The whole I planned.*
> *Youth shows but half: trust God; see all nor be afraid."*

Now — and to old age — and beyond, we trust; we want to see all; and we are not afraid, O God of the eternal! Amen.

* * * * *

(In his *Papirer X 3 A 711,* Kierkegaard has written, "So you are immortal. Do not give your self the trouble of doubting it or even of trying to prove it. You are immortal. You go on to the hereafter, and eternity is not the land of shadows, but of light, of transparence, where nothing is hidden, but held up to the light, and it is the same as in confession. Think of it closely. You are alone before God, and he is all light; he inhabits a light which none can penetrate, but he is a light that can penetrate everything. Oh! Take hold of that moment so that you might reveal yourself entirely." In his *Journal* he adds, "Father in Heaven! When You at the last reveal Yourself completely, let us not awaken in Your presence like a frightened bird that flies about in dismay, but like a child waking from its sleep with a heavenly smile.")

Father in Heaven! Was it right of that gloomy prophet to speak of "grim death, our last great foe?" Was the poet mistaken when he wrote, "Twilight and evening bell, and after that the dark"? Is it in "the valley of death" where You promised to walk with us on our last earthly stroll? No, Your promise was that You would walk with us "through the valley of the *shadow* of death." Shadows are not real things; shadows cannot harm us. Yes, they may startle and frighten, but there is no real harm in that. If there are shadows as we approach that fearsome valley, it is because there is a light somewhere, for there cannot be shadows without light. There *is* a light beckoning us on — and that Light, my Lord, is the Light that lights the path of everyone who comes into this world, the Light for everyone of us as we leave this world! May we greet the Light for everyone of us as we leave this world! May we greet the Light at the other end of that valley, not as the startled bird that flutters up at the sudden breaking of the dawn, but as the happy child awaking from sleep with a heavenly smile and shouting, "Hello, world!" May we awake in Your likeness and sing, "Hello, New World!" Help us to live each day as though we were living in Your Heavenly Kingdom, Your New World — here! — and guide us to live *now* as though it were already forever, for it is! Help us to remember always that we are only sojourners in this land which You have given us and that it will be no new or strange experience to greet that day which finds us "homeward bound!" Amen.

*   *   *   *   *

(One observation about prayer that Kierkegaard repeats again and again is that it is not possible to say "an unreserved Amen" to a prayer any more than it is possible to speak of the end of love. True love never ends. Also, there never comes a true end of the prayer that is prayed sincerely and zealously, for, with all our dedication and trust, we can never say that all our needs are expressed nor has all that is in our hearts been manifested, even before God. He explains (in *Papirer IX A 24*): "How rare it is to be able to say an unreserved *Amen* to a prayer! How rarely, if ever, has this happened even to someone who habitually prays with zeal and perseverance! It is even more rare than that moment of love where lovers are absolutely one another's ideal. To say *Amen* so that there is not a word, not a single word to add; when *Amen* is that unique word which satisfies and fulfills! To have prayed so that every need is satisfied in the outpouring of prayer, so that we have said all that was in our hearts, to have said it completely, that is, to have become transparent to ourselves before God, in all our weakness, but also in all our hope! Oh! There are moments, and you have perhaps felt them often enough. There are moments when the treasures of language seem insufficient to express what you feel in your heart of hearts. But now this would be the opposite of such a moment; all the words of our language would be superfluous. What if they have all been forgotten? They are no longer needed. There is nothing to add but the *Amen.*" SK expresses for us all our inexpressible gratitude for the incomprehensible largesse of prayer when he writes, "Oh, when I think upon all that has been vouchsafed me, the greater my desire for an eternity in which to thank God!")

It is true, O Lord: You have told us to pray without ceasing. There is no other way we can pray, our Father, for constantly we are aware of how quickly we can stray, how ready we are to doubt, how easily we can be beguiled and misled, how devastatingly we fall short. You are the God of completeness, for all fulness dwells with You. Even at our fullest we feel empty and unfulfilled. Patience we lack; perseverance, too. How often we conclude that we have done all that we can, exhausted all the powers that we possess. Of a sudden we realize that it is not on *our* powers that we need to depend. It is not *our* wisdom that suffices for the world's need. All that matters is Thy goodness, Thy greatness, Thy graciousness. In the midst of life, we are in debt — in debt not only for Your blessings, which are beyond money and beyond price, but also for Your love which places all the ages in Your debt. Since it has been Your generosity to give more than we can ever desire or seek, we thank You above all for an eternity in which we can thank our God! Nor do we ever say an unreserved and final *Amen* to this or any prayer we pray, but continue to rejoice with never-ending gratitude and praise! Amen and Amen and Amen, on and on and on!

*   *   *   *   *

Acknowledgments

We express our deep gratitude to the following for assistance in this venture:

Det kongelige Bibliotek, Copenhagen, Denmark, for permission to translate and publish Kierkegaard's works

Jacob Thomsen, of The Royal Library, for his precious assistance and encouragement

William Cullen Bryant, for passage from "To a Waterfowl"

John Drinkwater, for the lines from his "A Prayer"

William Brighty Rand (a.k.a. Matthew Browne), for lines from his nursery rhyme (adapted)

Matthew Arnold, "Great Physician" lines, stanza 3 of his "Memorial Verses" (adapted)

Blaise Pascal, for lines suggested by his statement in Pensée 277: "The heart has reasons of which reason has no knowledge."

Bibliography

Bretall, Robert (Editor), *A Kierkegaard Anthology,* The Modern Library, New York, 1936

Colette, Jacques, *Kierkegaard, The Difficulty of Being Christian,* University of Notre Dame Press

Collins, James, *The Mind of Kierkegaard*, Henry Regnery Co., Chicago, 1953

Dru, Alexander, *The Journals of Kierkegaard,* Harper and Row, 1958

Gill, Jerry H., *Essays on Kierkegaard*, Burgess Publishing Company, Minneapolis, Minnesota, 1969

Hubben, William, *Four Prophets of Our Destiny,* The Macmillan Co., New York, 1962

LaFarge, Rene, *Jean-Paul Sartre: His Philosophy,* University of Notre Dame Press, 1967

Martin, H. V., *Kierkegaard, the Melancholy Dane,* Philosophical Library, New York

Rohde, Peter, *Soren Kierkegaard,* George Allen & Unwin, Ltd., London, 1963

Smith, Ronald Gregor (Editor), *The Last Years, Journals 1853-1858,* Harper & Row

Thompson, Josiah, *Kierkegaard*, Alfred A. Knopf, New York, 1973